KU-792-134

▪ JOURNEY THROUGH ▪
NAMIBIA

JOURNEY THROUGH
NAMIBIA

MOHAMED AMIN · DUNCAN WILLETTS · TAHIR SHAH

Camerapix Publishers International
NAIROBI

Acknowledgements:

We would like to thank the many organizations and people throughout Namibia who gave us help and advice in the production of this book, in particular Wilfred Sentefol and Irmtraut Biederlack of South-West Africa Safaris, Chris Schutte of Namibia Commercial Aviation, Kobus Grobbelaar of Air Namibia, Dennis and Rosalind Rundle, Ulenga Ben Ulenga, Deputy Minister of the Ministry of Wildlife, Conservation and Tourism, and Amy Schoeman. We also wish to thank Carol Morgan of Namib-Sun Hotels and Mani Goldbeck for their contributions.

Our thanks, also, to John Reader for his diamond photographs on pages 1,37, 38, 39 and 40 and to Amy Schoeman for her photographs on pages 5 and 121.

We also wish to pay special tribute to the late Louw Schoeman, who died during the production of this book, for his many kindnesses and inspiration. His contributions included flights for aerial photography along the stunning Skeleton Coast.

And finally we must thank all the people of Namibia who made us so welcome.

First published 1994 by
Camerapix Publishers International,
P.O. Box 45048,
Nairobi, Kenya

ISBN 1 874041 23 7

This book was designed and produced by
Camerapix Publishers International,
P.O. Box 45048,
Nairobi, Kenya

Edited by Amy Schoeman and Brian Tetley
Production Editor: Debbie Gaiger
Design: Craig Dodd

Printed in Hong Kong by South China Printing (1988) Limited.

End papers: Namibian tapestry depicting San Bushmen. Half title: Spectacular array of uncut diamonds from the Consolidated Diamond Mine at Oranjemund.Page 2: Sculpted trunks of acacia trees preserved by the Namib climate. These trees last flowered as long as 500 years ago. Title page: Twin-mirror reflections glow in eastern Caprivi as the sun sinks beneath the horizon. Contents page: Stark beauty of the majestic Roaring Dunes in Namibia's Skeleton Coast.

· CONTENTS ·

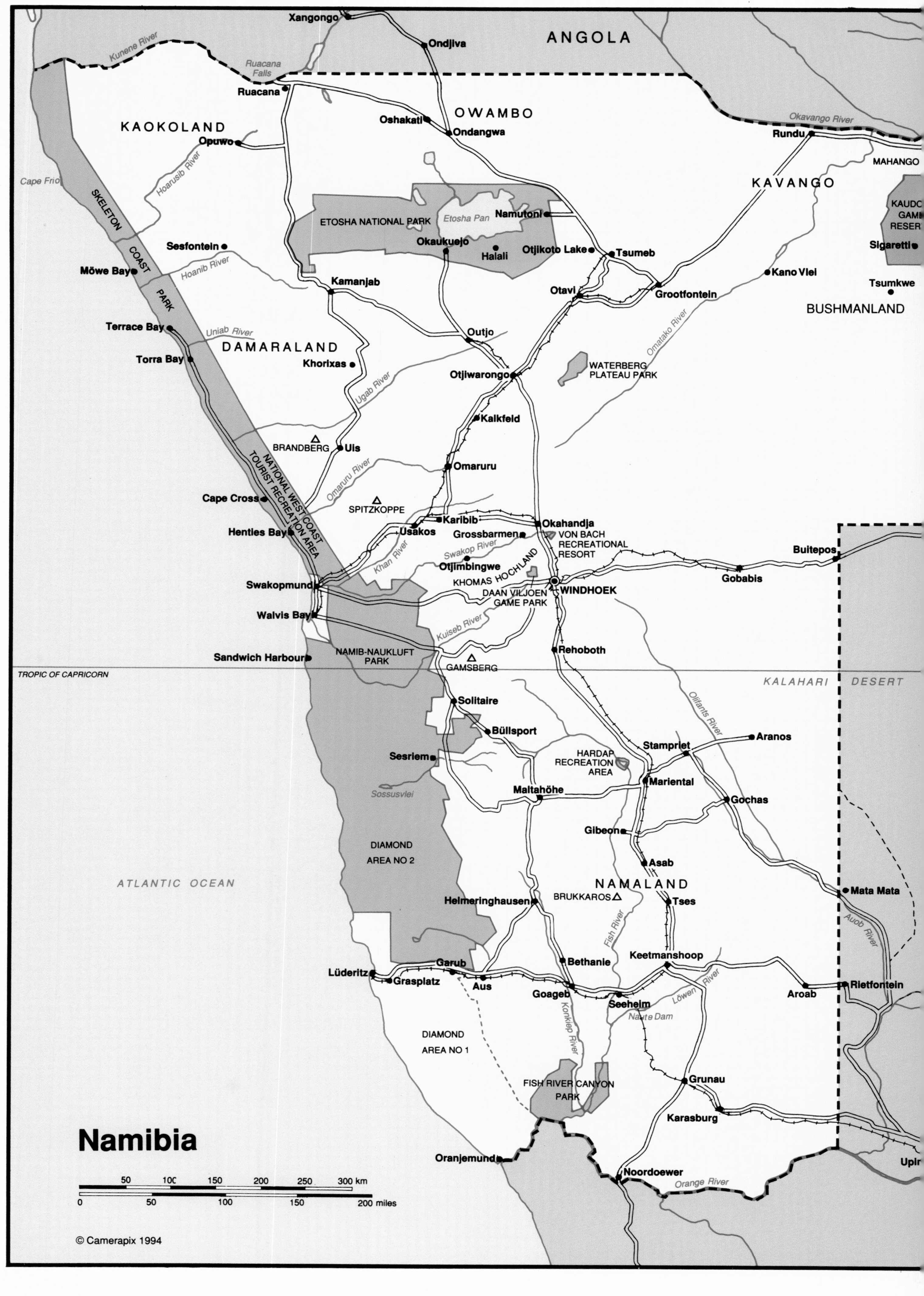

Xangongo
Ondjiva
ANGOLA
Kunene River
Ruacana Falls
Ruacana
OWAMBO
Oshakati
Ondangwa
KAOKOLAND
Opuwo
Okavango River
Rundu
MAHANGO
KAVANGO
Cape Frio
Hoarusib River
SKELETON COAST PARK
ETOSHA NATIONAL PARK
Etosha Pan
Namutoni
KAUDO GAME RESER
Okaukuejo
Halali
Otjikoto Lake
Tsumeb
Sigaretti
Sesfontein
Möwe Bay
Hoanib River
Kamanjab
Otavi
Grootfontein
Kano Vlei
Tsumkwe
BUSHMANLAND
Terrace Bay
Uniab River
Outjo
Omatako River
DAMARALAND
Torra Bay
Khorixas
Otjiwarongo
WATERBERG PLATEAU PARK
Ugab River
Kalkfeld
BRANDBERG
Uis
NATIONAL WEST COAST TOURIST RECREATION AREA
Omaruru
Omaruru River
Cape Cross
SPITZKOPPE
Karibib
Okahandja
Henties Bay
Usakos
Grossbarmen
VON BACH RECREATIONAL RESORT
Khan River
Swakop River
Otjimbingwe
KHOMAS HOCHLAND
Buitepos
Swakopmund
WINDHOEK
Gobabis
DAAN VILJOEN GAME PARK
Walvis Bay
Kuiseb River
Rehoboth
Sandwich Harbour
NAMIB-NAUKLUFT PARK
GAMSBERG
TROPIC OF CAPRICORN
KALAHARI DESERT
Solitaire
Büllsport
Olifants River
Stampriet
Aranos
Sesriem
HARDAP RECREATION AREA
Mariental
Sossusvlei
Maltahöhe
Gochas
Gibeon
DIAMOND AREA NO 2
Asab
ATLANTIC OCEAN
NAMALAND
Helmeringhausen
BRUKKAROS
Tses
Mata Mata
Fish River
Auob River
Keetmanshoop
Bethanie
Garub
Lüderitz
Grasplatz
Aus
Goageb
Seeheim
Löwen River
Aroab
Rietfontein
Naute Dam
Konkiep River
DIAMOND AREA NO 1
FISH RIVER CANYON PARK
Grunau
Karasburg
Namibia
Oranjemund
Noordoewer
Orange River
Upir
50 100 150 200 250 300 km
0 50 100 150 200 miles
© Camerapix 1994

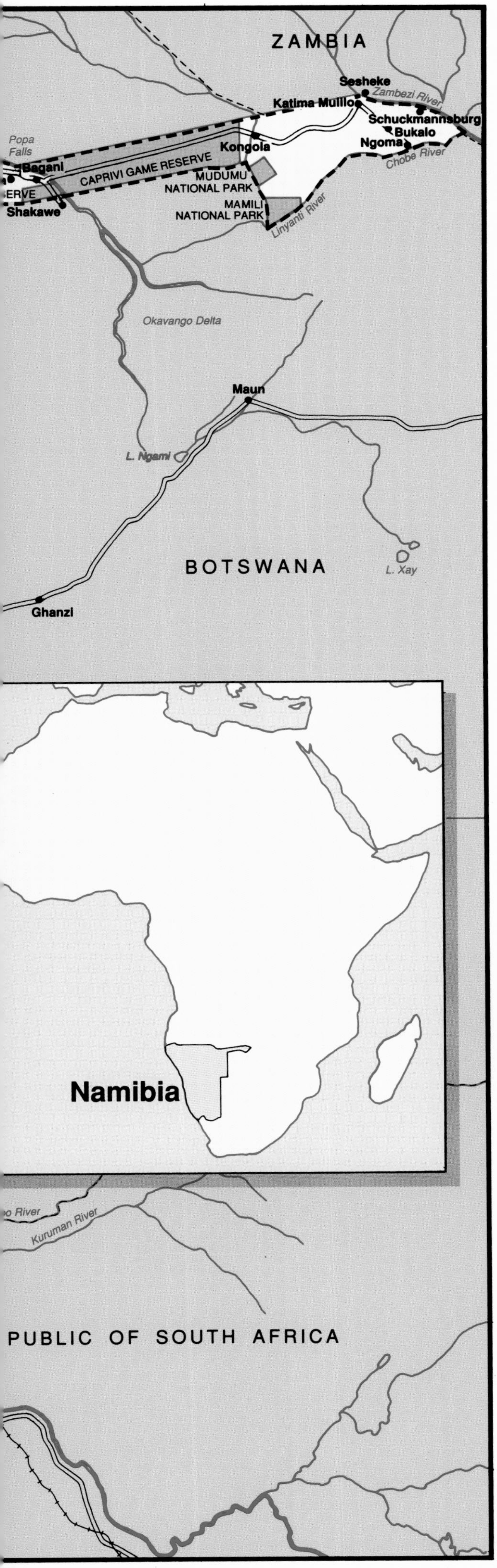

ZAMBIA
Sesheke
Zambezi River
Katima Mulilo
Schuckmannsburg
Bukalo
Ngoma
Chobe River
Popa Falls
Bagani
CAPRIVI GAME RESERVE
Kongola
MUDUMU NATIONAL PARK
MAMILI NATIONAL PARK
Linyanti River
ERVE
Shakawe
Okavango Delta
Maun
L. Ngami
BOTSWANA
L. Xay
Ghanzi
Namibia
o River
Kuruman River
PUBLIC OF SOUTH AFRICA

Katima Mulilo
CAPRIVI
OMUSATI
OHANGWENA
Opuwo
Oshakati
OSHIKOTO
Rundu
OKAVANGO
OSHANA
Tsumeb
KUNENE
OTJOZONDJUPA
Otjiwarongo
OMAHEKE
ERONGO
Gobabis
Swakopmund
WINDHOEK
KHOMAS
HARDAP
Mariental
Keetmanshoop
KARAS

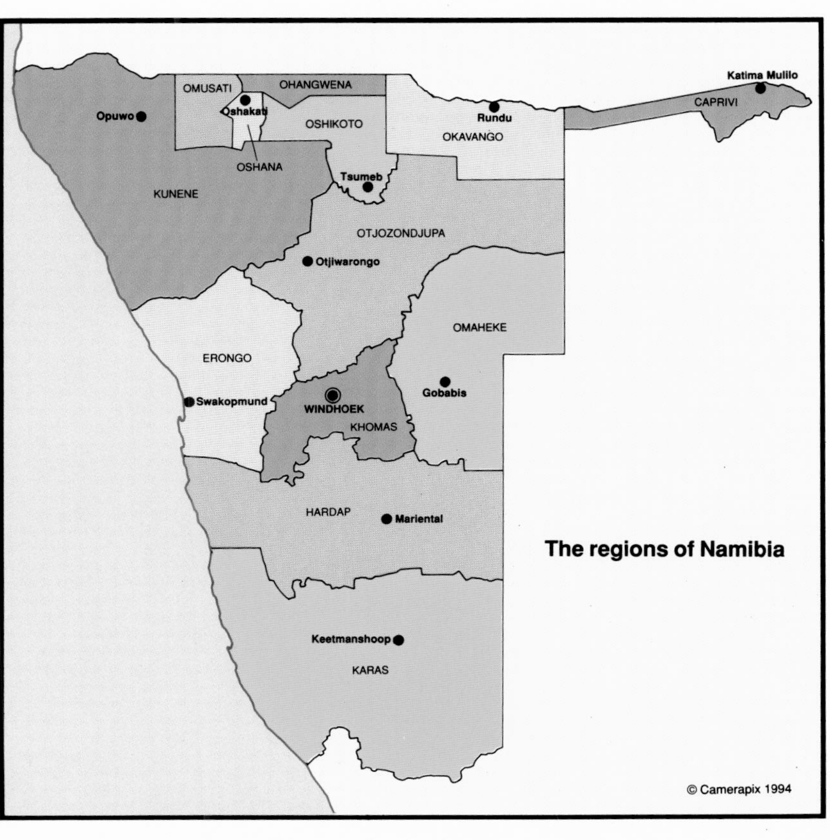

The regions of Namibia

INTRODUCTION

JOURNEY THROUGH NAMIBIA

Previous pages: Unearthly images of light, shade and abstract form created by the shadowed valleys, ridges and crests of the wind-driven sand mountains in the Namib Desert.

Namibia is one of Africa's youngest and most mysterious nations; a land of daunting size and rugged beauty. Within its realm contrasts abound. Rocky plateaux rise hard by expansive deserts; lush watercourses give way to barren vistas and ancient peoples brush with modern technology.

In Namibia's vast desert regions some of the world's most enduring plants, creatures and peoples abide according to an archaic natural scheme. Into these endless tracts, nature cast her richest treasures — diamonds, other precious stones and minerals. Today the country accounts for roughly one-sixth of the world's diamond wealth.

Records from the time of Herodotus indicate that the Phoenicians were the first explorers to circumnavigate the African continent. They were followed, around 600 BC, by a fleet despatched by the Egyptian Pharaoh, Necho II, whose ships sailed along the continent's eastern seaboard.

But not until 2,000 years later, when Portuguese navigators and explorers set out in search of new lands — and a sea route to the Indies — did the continent begin to yield its secrets. In the fifteenth century, King John II of Portugal sent two expeditions under Diego Cão to Africa's western seaboard. History records that the explorer anchored south of what is now Namibia's Skeleton Coast and stepped ashore to set up a stone cross on top of a rocky cape. The cross stood for more than 400 years until the captain of a German vessel removed it late last century and took it to a museum in Berlin. Two years after Diego Cão left his cruciform, Bartholomeo Diaz, another Portuguese explorer, positioned a second cross in a bay he named *Angra Pequena*, Little Bay, now Lüderitz Bay.

Looking at the formidable dunes of the great Namib Desert as they tumble into the icy Atlantic, it is not difficult to understand why so few voyagers chose to venture inland. The oldest desert in the world — some eighty million years — the Namib seems denuded of life, scorched by noonday sun, cooled by chill night mists that billow in from the ocean shutting out the frosty moon. Yet, astonishingly, life exists above and below its surface as plants and creatures draw sustenance from the wind and moisture of its misty phantoms. Such life, from tiny beetles to mighty elephants, have made this improbable wilderness their home. Indeed, many species are found nowhere else in the world. Swept by searing winds, the highest dunes in the world — mountains of sand — roll across the desert like roaming clouds to meet at a place called Sossusvlei.

East of the Namib stand remnants of the time before man walked these lands — dinosaur tracks and petrified forests, the greatest meteorite on earth and ancient castles of clay. From the eroded cliffs of Fish River Canyon, through Namibia's quaint, colonial-style towns, to the wild expanses of Etosha and the Caprivi Strip, Namibia's brittle beauty is vast even by African standards. Yet, although its 824,268 square kilometres is four times the size of Britain, its population numbers fewer than one and a half million people, giving it one of

Opposite: Declared a national monument in 1950, the Petrified Forest in Damaraland is thought to be 260 million years old. The trees probably grew elsewhere before being swept downstream by floodwaters to their present position.

Above: Rock engravings of human footprints in Namibia's treasury of prehistoric art.

the lowest population densities in the world with fewer than two people to each square kilometre. This remarkably low number may ensure that the changes ravaging much of Africa never affect its latest republic.

Basking in summer temperatures — that range from 10-33°C between October and April and from 6-26°C in winter between May and September — Namibia's unspoilt splendour makes it truly a land of the free for the free. A developing network of well-maintained tar, gravel and dirt roads allows visitors to reach the farthest corners of what has been called Africa's Gem — from the fallen glory of the rocky Finger of God in the south to the majesty of the Okavango River and the rapids of the Popa Falls in the north; from the mystery of the White Lady of the Brandberg to the raw power of the Namib Desert; from the gigantic fossil woods of the Petrified Forest near Khorixas to the Hoba Meteorite near Grootfontein; from the abundant wildlife of that other Eden, Etosha National Park, to the fascination of the Skeleton Coast.

And its people, every bit as unique and colourful, include perhaps Africa's oldest race, the San Bushmen whose affinity to the trackless desert and savannahs where they live seems almost miraculous. One of their legends underlines this unlikely symbiosis: 'Now you come, now you go. When you come again you will never go.'

The many African tribes and European settlers live in a country of contrasts and vibrant colour. It is bordered in the west by the mighty Atlantic whose shores are lined by the Namib-Naukluft Park which sprawls across almost 50,000 square kilometres, an area larger than Denmark. The southern border with South Africa is formed by the Orange River. In the north, much of the

Above: Detail of prehistoric rock carving in the Stone Age art treasury discovered at Twyfelfontein.

border between Namibia and Angola is made up of the Kunene and Okavango Rivers. And to the east lies the Kalahari Desert which sweeps into Botswana.

Many contemporary aspects of Namibia bear witness to the Victorian age when the European powers carved up Africa. Even now, Herero women dress in Victorian fashions while the charming buildings of both Swakopmund and Windhoek, the capital, reflect nineteenth-century convention and style. These incongruous vestiges extend beyond costume or architecture to the national boundaries where two particular instances remain curious reminders of colonial days. The first is a narrow corridor of land, 482 kilometres long, extending as far as the Zambezi. The Caprivi Strip, so named after Baron von Caprivi, the German Chancellor of the time, is also known as the Devil's Finger. It was the outcome of the German Kaiser's ambition to join his western and eastern African empires together. The second anachronism, Walvis Bay, midway between the Kunene and Orange Rivers, was annexed in 1878 to become part of Britain's Cape Colony, yet it remained under South African jurisdiction until the end of 1992, when Namibia began to share in its administration.

Namibia forms three distinct topographical regions — the Namib Desert; the central inland plateau's mountains and plains with, most magnificent of all, Etosha National Park; and finally the Kalahari Desert in the south-east reaches of the country.

The Kalahari's western counterpart, the Namib Desert, stretches more than 2,000 kilometres along the African coast in an arid band between 150 and 200 kilometres wide. In these virtually waterless conditions, its unique animals and plants take their moisture from the cool mists that sweep in from the Atlantic.

Opposite: Sunlight pierces the gloom of Sesriem Canyon: a gorge up to 30 metres in depth carved by the once mighty waters of the Tsauchab River.

Above: Blooming thorn tree brings a splash of colour to the arid environment of Etosha National Park.

The roving dunes along the southern tract of coast are older than any other in the world. To the north lies the legendary Skeleton Coast where the sun-bleached bones of sailors and whales lie side by side with rusting shipwrecks. There, the Namib's dunes are complemented by vast, hard-baked granite flats which stretch from one horizon to the next.

What little takes root in the way of vegetation must rank among the world's most unusual and enduring plants, chief of which is a remarkable dwarf tree that dates back to prehistoric times. Some existing specimens of the tree — *Welwitschia mirabilis* — are more than 2,000 years old. Other marvels have also adapted ingeniously to this cruel land and manage to survive the scorching daytime heat and freezing night temperatures.

Several rivers, most of them seasonal, flow westwards into the Atlantic along Namibia's 1,600-kilometre-long seaboard — from the northernmost Kunene River to the Orange River in the extreme south. Three major towns dominate the seaboard. In summertime, elegant Swakopmund, halfway between Angola and South Africa, is woken from its hibernation by masses of tourists who double its wintertime population. A little to the south, Walvis Bay, the deepest harbour on Africa's south-west coast, is another popular haven for tourists. The port serves freight and fishing vessels.

The port of Lüderitz, with its fairy-tale architecture, almost 500 kilometres south of Walvis Bay, has been in use since Bartholomeo Diaz moored there in the fifteenth century. East of Walvis Bay, the Namib-Naukluft Park stretches far inland, culminating in dramatic 305-metre mountains of sand at Sossusvlei.

However, the most spectacular feature of the southern region is the deep cleft in the earth's surface, the Fish River Canyon, a colossal gorge more than 160 kilometres long.

On its eastern flank, the Namib Desert meets Namibia's immense inland plateau, the nation's second distinct topographical region, which forms the country's south-north backbone. This varies from brooding mountains with jagged 2,440-metre peaks to wide plains and sandy valleys. Amid the high mountains at Namibia's northernmost extremities, the Kunene and Okavango Rivers flow all year round, the latter feeding the Okavango Delta in neighbouring Botswana.

And it is there in the north, close to the Angolan border, that you find Namibia's most magical landscape — the wilderness wonderlands of Etosha National Park. One of the world's largest game parks, Etosha's 22,270 square kilometres — bigger than Wales — know no seasons. As day melts into night, so the weeks and months merge into one. The Etosha Pan, which gives the park its name, covers some 6,000 square kilometres in the east. This dry pan used to be the lake into which the Kunene River emptied itself, but following continental shifting, and the subsequent diversion of the Kunene's course to the Atlantic

Above: Windhoek's 1907 Villa Migliarina attests to Namibia's colonial heritage.

Ocean, the pan became what it is today. This immense shallow bowl, which fills only occasionally after the onset of the rains, is all that remains of that ancient lake. It is the source and sustenance of all life at Etosha, whose plains are home to a variety of creatures — birds, game animals and insects — some of which are found nowhere else in the world. As the scorching heat bakes the bleached and seemingly endless plains, these animals make their way to the rapidly dwindling waterholes in the pan to quench their thirst.

The land between Etosha and Windhoek, the capital city, is dotted with a host of small towns, such as Grootfontein and Otjiwarongo, where you can enjoy the distinctive charms of Namibian society. The most densely populated region of Namibia is Owambo, where the great majority of people live in rural settings.

Windhoek lies almost at the centre of Namibia, linked to the main urban areas and neighbouring countries by an extensive and expanding infrastructure.

Above: More than ninety per cent of southern Africa's salt is recovered from the waters of the Atlantic Ocean by evaporation in massive man-made lagoons near Walvis Bay.

The capital's charm — buildings of colonial German design, and modern skyscrapers — is enhanced by its location close to the Auas and Eros Mountains and not far from the Khomas Hochland in the west.

East of Windhoek, the boundless Kalahari Desert, which stretches southwards down the country's eastern flank straddling the border with Botswana, forms Namibia's third distinct landscape, surprisingly different from its western counterpart. For, unlike the Namib, the Kalahari is comparatively rich in plants and grasses, and sustains a great variety of life. Camel-thorn, red ebony and silver terminalia trees, mix with a wide range of shrubs and succulents, providing welcome shade and refreshment for the people and creatures that live in the desert.

Keetmanshoop, the largest town at the edge of the Kalahari, grew up in the south around a mission station which later became a German military garrison.

Long before the Europeans first sailed along Africa's south-west coast,

Namibia's people enjoyed their ancient ways and age-old beliefs following a destiny diverted only by the first footsteps of western navigators, explorers, missionaries and carpet-baggers.

Belonging to eleven groups, a rich tapestry of tribes and peoples has endowed Namibia with its striking and varied cultural legacy. These myriad people have become as one in their new-found freedom. Yet each group retains a distinctive character and language, setting it apart from its neighbours.

Under the old, pre-independence South African administration, these cultures were demarcated geographically by a series of ethnic "homelands" — such as Kaokoland, Owambo, Kavango, Bushmanland, Hereroland and Damaraland. But these were swept away in 1990 by a new local government structure that divided Namibia into thirteen regional authorities, each with its own political constituencies.

Almost one-tenth of Namibia's people, many of them European, make their home in Windhoek. In the few years since independence, the pace of migration from rural areas into the towns and city, spurred by the relentless drought that ravaged southern Africa at the end of the 1980s and in the early 1990s, quickened. Peasants, labourers and village folk flocked to the capital in search of jobs and food.

Namibia's original citizens, long before the other groups migrated to the south-west of the continent, are the San Bushmen. They once occupied the whole of southern Africa; their language is similar to that of their South African kith and kin, the Nama. Fine-boned and lightly coloured, these hunter-gatherers, a nomadic people skilled in bushcraft and survival in the harshest conditions, are thought to have roamed Namibia's wildernesses thousands of years ago. Their rock paintings, in caves and on cliffs throughout the country, depict San life, hunting, and the animals around them. For centuries they roamed free at peace with nature. It was only when they came in contact with outside influences that disaster struck — with the influx of Nama pastoralists, themselves descendants of the Khoikhoi of the Cape Province. This invasion during the early eighteenth century was a tragedy for these peaceful people — and it was compounded when the Wambo and Damara tribes swept in behind the Nama while the Bantu-speaking Herero filtered into the Kaokoveld in north-west Namibia, before moving down the centre of the country. Finally, large numbers of the Oorlam tribe, themselves Nama who had closer contact with Western influences in the Cape, advanced into Namibia's heartlands. They brought with them weapons as well as a form of the Dutch language from the European communities in southern Africa. This dialect later became Afrikaans, which is still spoken widely in Namibia. It allows communication between the many indigenous tribes found in the country. Many customs and traditions have since been devastated and Namibia's extraordinary cultural heritage is

Above: Like an ancient sentinel, this replica cross stands guard over Lüderitz Peninsula on Diaz Point. It replaces the original erected by Bartholomeo Diaz on 25 July, 1488.

Above: Stained glass windows of Lüderitz's Evangelical Lutheran Church, Felsenkirche — known as the Church on the Rocks — were a gift from Kaiser Wilhelm II of Germany.

now under threat from modernization and development. But a few remain, as yet untrammelled by Western influence, thus preserving the country's unique legacy.

Namibia has about 70,000 European citizens, most of whom speak Afrikaans, while others are mainly of German or English descent. There are many Namibians of mixed race, known as coloureds.

The Wambo tribe's 800,000 people, the largest single group, live in the region between Etosha and Angola. To the north-east, Okavango is home to the 180,000 people of the Kavango tribe, the second largest group. Three tribes — the Herero, Himba and Mbanderu — form the 90,000 people of what was Hereroland in Otjozondjupa, which lies to the south of Okavango. During German rule the Herero were almost decimated. Many now roam Windhoek and other towns selling trinkets, or surviving how they can.

The home of the Tjimba and Himba tribes, who are related to the Herero, was

Above: Wildlife trophies adorn the wall of Lüderitz Museum alongside a portrait of Bartholomeo Diaz, the ill-fated Portuguese navigator, and memorabilia of Adolf Lüderitz, after whom the town was named.

Kaokoveld in Kunene. Scorning materialism and the trappings of modern civilization, much like the Maasai of East Africa, the Himba have become a fascination for Western observers intrigued by their traditional way of life. They were forced into their empty wastelands during the last century by the Nama tribe.

Erongo — where the Damara people endure a harsh existence — is part of the old Damaraland. It is thought the Damara travelled southwards from western Africa through the centre of the continent in a migration lasting many centuries, bringing with them the secrets of extracting iron and making pottery.

The homelands of the Nama lie in the south in Karas, an area dominated by the Orange River. Until the end of the eighteenth century the Nama were at peace. But that was shattered by a massive influx of Herero in search of grazing. The war between the Herero and the Nama lasted for decades and claimed thousands of victims. The most tragic of all Western influences were the

Following pages: Brightly-coloured hot air balloon provides sharp focus to the beautiful yet barren landscape of the Namib-Naukluft National Park.

Above: Swakopmund's museum is filled with relics from Namibia's German colonial rule. The exhibits range from primitive dentistry tools to the skull of a San warrior.

firearms brought in by the bellicose Oorlam who propelled South West Africa into an era of unprecedented confrontation. The half-caste Baster people were driven northwards by the Boers in the 1860s across the Orange River to settle south of what is now Windhoek in the Hardap Region. These protracted migrations over vast areas laid the foundations for today's Namibian cultures. But it was a period characterised by open warfare as tribes found themselves competing for land and scarce resources. Whole generations perished but little was accomplished, except to consolidate the colonialist stranglehold over the land and its people.

Namibia's long history is also stained with the bloodshed from white domination — a tide of terror and belligerence that may never be erased entirely from Namibian soil.

Even before the nineteenth century, Europe's superpowers vied for supremacy of south-western Africa's strategic bays and inlets. To thwart other

V5-HAA

Opposite: Lioness in postprandial pose shades herself from the extreme heat of Etosha's afternoon.

Above: Oryx, the hardiest of all antelopes, take water at one of Etosha National Park's perennial waterholes against a rocky backdrop of thorn-tree woodlands.

roving European forces seeking to expand their control of Africa's western flank, the Dutch seized Walvis Bay and Lüderitz Bay in 1793. But when the British took control of the Cape of Good Hope two years later, they also took possession of Walvis Bay and a string of other key locations.

Few Europeans, if any, ventured into the heart of Namibia — it was far too dangerous. The great quests came with the onset of the nineteenth century. The first sorties into Namibia's interior were made by a small corps of hardy explorers, such as Pieter Pienaar who ventured inland by way of rivers like the Swakop. It was not until the arrival of the missionaries, however, that the first major expeditions were accomplished. Among the many Christian pioneers the names of Abraham and Christian Albrecht, who lived with the Nama and stopped at nothing to spread their faith, ring loudest. Johann Heinrich Schmelen, another Christian missionary, was an extraordinary man who took a Nama bride and set her to work translating the Bible into Nama. The London

Above: Grave of an unknown soldier at a cemetery in Windhoek. The monument is fashioned in the distinctive form of the German military honour, the Knight's Cross.

Missionary Society focused on what is now the Caprivi Strip where the most famous of all missionaries, David Livingstone, was stationed between 1850 and 1851. All across Namibia missionaries spread the word, settling among the Nama, Herero, Wambo and other tribes.

But the Christian message did nothing to prevent the conflicts which rent the final years of the last century. British attempts to end inter-tribal rivalry were feeble, mainly because they had no wish to become enmeshed. And when Adolf Lüderitz, a trader from Bremen, appealed to the Kaiser to do something in 1882, Bismarck decided to act. He annexed the whole of what is now Namibia, except for Walvis Bay and some small islands which the British retained.

At first the small German colonial administration operated a policy of *laissez-faire*. But as the bloodshed between tribes continued, the Germans cut supplies of arms and ammunition, built forts and brought in a military corps, the *Schutztruppe*. In 1904 these cold-blooded killers instigated a reign of terror in

Above: Windhoek memorial to the fallen soldiers of two world wars.

which most of the 80,000-strong Herero men, women and children were slaughtered. By the end of 1907 the tribe counted their numbers in hundreds.

This ethnic slaughter preceded the discovery of a rich diamond field by railway worker Zacharias Lewala, a former miner from South Africa's Kimberley diamond mines. One day, in April 1908, he was shovelling drifting sand from the line near Grasplatz Station, when he noticed the telltale twinkle of a diamond. Lewala scooped up the glistening stone and gave it to his boss, August Stauch, a German railway inspector. Stauch immediately staked a claim to that piece of desert. It came to be called Kolmanskop. The news spread like fire and, within weeks, dozens of prospectors had pegged out the entire area south-east of Lüderitz. De Beers, the great South African diamond conglomerate, eager to protect its markets, played down suggestions that the deposits were worth anything, while the colonial administration gave mining concessions only to German syndicates. Prisoners-of-war from the Herero

Above: A Cessena 310 — part of Namibia Commercial Aviation's seventeen plane charter fleet. NCA operate throughout Namibia and to all the neighbouring countries.

rebellion were used as slave labour as there were no Africans in the diamond zone. Diamond fever continued and new fields were constantly being discovered, particularly in the first two decades of the century. Driven by diamond wealth, the colony's economy grew swiftly. Business expanded and roads, railways and port facilities developed. By 1913, one-fifth of all Africa's mined diamonds came from Namibia.

But at the height of this unparalleled prosperity, German South West Africa became embroiled in World War I. Isolated from the German empire, far from any defensive resources, it was at the mercy of the British forces. But South Africa delayed the push into German South West Africa until the 1914 Boer rebellion was quelled.

Then, in January 1915, South African forces — under the British flag — landed at Swakopmund and Lüderitz. Vastly outnumbered, the Germans surrendered within six months — on 9 July, 1915. It was the first German colony

Above: Familiar Windhoek landmark is the equestrian memorial to mounted troops who carried out bitter reprisals against native rebellions during the early years of German colonialisation.

to be captured by British forces and a new administration was installed at Windhoek.

But the change did nothing to lift the burden of oppression. Indeed it signalled yet another chapter in the colony's long history of suffering, one that lasted more than seven decades.

In 1919, under the newly-formed League of Nations, South West Africa, as Namibia now became known, was entrusted to South Africa as a mandated territory. The League's intentions could not be doubted. It prohibited South Africa from conscripting Africans into military service, and indeed ordered the trustees to advance the country's social and economic status. But the mandate failed to spell out the need for eventual self-government and this crucial omission allowed South Africa to treat the country as its own colony. In effect this permitted South Africa to plunder its resources and exploit its people. The interests of white South Africans were ever first, and the riches too good to miss. In 1920, Ernest Oppenheimer snapped up the diamond concessions from the nine German companies that operated the syndicate. He paid the bargain price of forty million marks and founded Consolidated Diamond Mines — CDM. In the first twelve years of mining, six and a half million carats of diamonds — a carat is 200 milligrams — were recovered.

Land was wealth, too, and now the Afrikaner settlers threw the peasants off the land to carve out farms on the rich grazing lands of the central plateau. Six years after the war ended the white population had doubled. By 1926, the indigenous occupiers of their native pastures had been forced out to make way for almost 1,000 white farms, each averaging about 37,000 acres. These reluctant itinerants were destined to wander semi-desert regions seeking pastures for their herds. Under apartheid, blacks and coloureds were forced to live away from white communities. Pretoria established a commission to map out tribal homelands. Known as the Odendaal Plan, after the commission's chairman, it divided the various tribes to prevent them from rebellion and insurgency. Homelands such as Kavango, Owambo and Damaraland, were created in the more overgrazed and overpopulated regions of Namibia, mainly in the northern wilderness. Residents could only leave if they found work in a white area under a white master.

Freedom for much of the rest of Africa dawned in the 1960s, however, and these new nations changed the balance of power within the United Nations. Their pressure put Namibia's plight on the world agenda. And, in October 1966, the United Nations ended the South African mandate, assuming responsibility for South West Africa under the United Nations Council for Namibia. But South Africa, which accused the UN of acting illegally, refused to relinquish power — sparking off a general strike and rebellions. South Africa responded with a state of emergency and imposed virtual martial law.

Air Namibia

Opposite: Golden skies of dawn welcome the Air Namibia 747 on its final approach to Windhoek's International Airport.

Above: Memorial to martyrs who died protesting their enforced resettlement from Windhoek's Old Location to the black township of Katutura.

At the start of the 1970s, the UN recognised the South West African People's Organization (SWAPO) as "the sole and authentic representative of the Namibian people". Under Shafiishuna Samuel Nujoma, SWAPO set out to unite all Namibians. Still South Africa refused to loosen its stranglehold.

It was Portugal's eventual departure from Africa as a colonial power in 1975 that acted as the real catalyst for freedom, giving SWAPO a platform in Angola from which to transform its insurrections into a full military offensive. Now Namibia's northern border provided sanctuary for SWAPO's guerrilla arm — the People's Liberation Army of Namibia (PLAN). South Africa labelled SWAPO as a communist organization, as most international support for SWAPO came from communist and Scandinavian countries. As a result, South Africa began a campaign of terror in northern Namibia, and thousands of refugees fled to Angola, Botswana and Zambia. Many of these exiles were recruited by PLAN, strengthening the fight for freedom. SWAPO broadened its

Opposite: Afterglow of a glorious Namibian sunset.

political support within Namibia by forging alliances with other political groups, and winning support from the churches. By the late 1970s, SWAPO was truly national, representing a complete cross-section of Namibian society. But in 1978 South Africa staged unrepresentative elections in Windhoek which were immediately condemned as "sham" by the United Nations.

To combat the thousands of troops which South Africa poured into northern Namibia, SWAPO needed a cohesive military strategy and coordinated initiatives. Roads were mined, ambushes laid and military bases raided.

The liberation war reached its height in the 1980s. Intense fighting in densely populated Owambo spread rapidly to Kavango and the barren Kaoko. PLAN also carried the war to other areas, including the central and southern regions — even Windhoek itself.

PLAN's spy-ring was extraordinarily skilled; the freedom fighters were given food, water, shelter and vital information, allowing raids to have the maximum impact. At the same time though, South Africa was able to infiltrate PLAN with spies of its own. SWAPO's discovery of this fact led to many innocent people being accused of spying for the enemy. As a result, South African military operations became increasingly brutal. Namibians were press-ganged into uniform and forced to take up arms against their own kin — while specialised terror units, *Koevoets,* were sent into battle.

Above: Office of the Prime Minister and Parliament buildings at Windhoek.

The war drained South Africa of billions of rands — and its enthusiasm for the fight. This war of thirty years, labelled by one side as a liberation struggle, and by the other as the attempted infiltration of communism, reached a stalemate. Neither side could win and it became clear other means of ending this conflict had to be found.

The 1988 agreement, which the Americans brokered between South Africa and Cuba to end the war in Angola, opened the door for Namibia's independence. Almost 50,000 refugees, the most distinguished of these being Samuel Nujoma himself, flooded back into the country for the November 1989 elections. The turnout was almost 100 per cent. SWAPO won a clear majority with 57.3 per cent of the vote giving them forty-one of the seventy-two seats in Namibia's fledgling parliament. They and the six other parties soon agreed on the constitution. Freedom for all — in religion, association, speech, thought and print — was guaranteed; and all discrimination outlawed.

Finally, on the night of 21 March 1990, after a struggle that had lasted well over a century, thousands of Namibians watched as the proud flag of their new nation was unfurled for the first time. And in the presence of UN Secretary General Dr. Javier Perez de Cuellar, and world leaders, Dr. Sam Nujoma became the first President of Namibia.

2 · ORANGE

RIVER, DIAMOND DESERT

Previous pages: Consecrated in 1912, Lüderitz's imposing Evangelical Lutheran Church, Felsenkirche — known as the Church on the Rocks — commands the heights of Lüderitz looking across to the harbour and Atlantic Ocean.

Opposite: Man and machine scour the diamond fields of Oranjemund, at the south-west extreme of Namibia.

There are few better places to begin a *Journey through Namibia* than at Noordoewer on the banks of the great Orange River. It is there that the main Namibian highway begins its run north. Wedged between the ever-shifting sands of the Namib to the west and the Kalahari's desert tundra to the east, southern Namibia is a barren but beautiful place, with some of Africa's most spectacular landscapes. Few people live there and the plants and creatures have had to adapt to life in a harsh, dry terrain. At the first flush of rain, however, the parched landscape turns lush green.

The Orange River, which flows more than 2,000 kilometres from its source in the Drakensberg Mountains of South Africa, forms Namibia's southern boundary with South Africa. It was on the southern banks of the river, in 1866, that young Erasmus Jacobs discovered a diamond. He had no idea what it was, but when he was found playing with it, diamond fever swept southern Africa. A series of finds fuelled a frenzy of greed, excitement and prospecting. The very fact that diamonds were accessible in the area was due to a natural process which happened millennia before. The Orange River — which once flowed from the interior of South Africa — cut into a Kimberlite pipe, the substance in which diamonds occur. The inherent hardness of the diamonds ensured that they survived the journey to the mouth of the Orange River, from where they were deposited along the Namibian coast.

As early as 1897, the master of a sailing vessel, Captain R. Jones, sailed into the harbour at Cape Town clutching a packet of diamonds. He claimed to have picked them up on one of the many islands along the southern coast of South West Africa. Again, in 1905 and 1906, a few diamonds were found in guano which had been mined on the same offshore islands. Two years later the first diamond fields were discovered, well north of the Orange River, at a remote spot on the Atlantic fringes of the Namib called Kolmanskop.

They brought rapid change and swift development. Hamlets turned into villages, villages blossomed into towns and roads and railways were laid. When the diamond seams around Kolmanskop began to run out during the late 1920s, operations were transferred to the diamond fields at the south-eastern edge of the Namib. And prospecting moved south to the Orange River. It was thought that as diamonds had been discovered at Alexander Bay, on the Orange River's southern banks, the seam should extend to the northern banks. Theory became fact in 1928 when geologists discovered more diamond coastal terraces north of the Orange River.

Diamonds, which the ancient Greeks believed were fragments of stars that had fallen to earth, are the key to the future of this young nation. They are also the reason for the existence of the small town of Oranjemund, founded by Consolidated Diamond Mines — CDM — in 1936 at the mouth of the Orange River. The town plays an important role in the Namibian economy — having

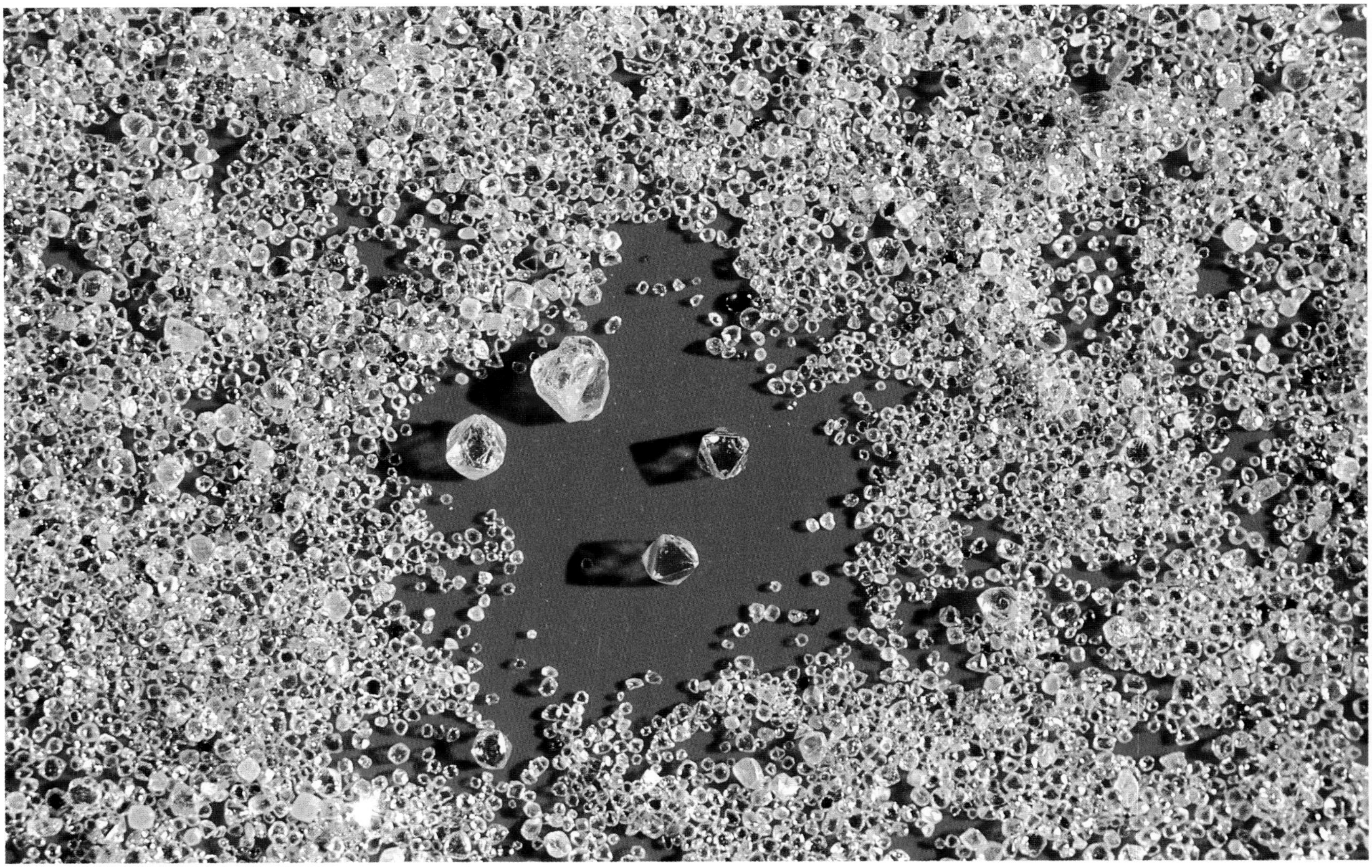

Opposite: Nature's booty, a hoard of polished gems unearthed in Namibia's rich soils.

Above: Diamonds are mined, graded and cut in Namibia.

replaced Lüderitz as mining headquarters in 1943. Complete with airport, rail and bus terminals, verdant municipal parks and immaculate golf course, Oranjemund is the closest thing to heaven in a harsh and intimidating land. It is a town of 8,000 residents without jobless or homeless people, where all medical treatment is free, and the company pumps water from the Orange River. With 5,000 workers Consolidated Diamond Mines is the country's largest employer, and in recent years, has established new mines at Auchas, on the banks of the Orange River, and Elizabeth Bay, just south of Lüderitz.

The depression of the 1930s and World War II reduced demand for diamonds. The world market did not recover until the 1950s. By the 1970s the mines were working flat-out with two million carats processed in 1977 alone. The Orange River and the Namib have been generous with their bounty, holding on to these precious gems, cast there by ancient tides, for man to recover by strip mining.

The *Sperrgebiet* — Forbidden Area — where these diamonds lie, is a daunting barrier of black, craggy cliffs with razor-sharp ridges and spectacular rock formations, including the 58-metre natural arch of Bogenfels rock. Because of its wealth, the coast is prohibited territory to all but mine officials and workers. Dykes are built to recover diamonds below the tideline when the waters of the lagoons that form are pumped dry. Mechanical diggers remove thirty million tonnes of earth, sand and rock a year at Oranjemund alone. The diggings, spread over several hundred square kilometres, form one of the world's largest open-cast mines.

Few sights are as awesome as those of the giant excavators, the largest and most spectacular earth-movers in the world, gouging great chunks of sand and rock out of the earth down to a depth of twenty-four metres, as protective dykes hold back the ever-threatening waters of the Atlantic. When the sand and rock are pulled away, the diamond-bearing gravels are revealed and a task force of Wambo labourers, armed with simple brooms, industriously sweep forward. They search the surface for diamonds lodged in tiny cracks and crevasses — retrieving an average of 6,000 carats of diamonds a day.

The scale of the operation can be perceived in the fact that for just 200 milligrams of diamond, at least thirteen-and-a-quarter tonnes of sand, gravel and conglomerate, have to be cleared away. These operations cost in the region of a million US dollars a day.

The biggest diamond ever recovered weighed 246 carats. Such wealth creates its own temptations and security within the forbidden territory is a continual battle. The theft of uncut diamonds is a massive industry on its own. For every three million dollars-worth of gemstones recovered, experts estimate that another ninety per cent finds its way onto the market.

Opposite: Rarest of rare, diamonds are Namibia's most important export.

Thieves use all manner of means to smuggle out their loot. Once, X-ray machines detected a condom containing 200 stones — while cut-away heels in shoes, hollow books and luggage handles have become commonplace discoveries to eagle-eyed security staff. Not long ago a homing pigeon was seen fluttering on a three-metre security fence; closer examination showed it was carrying a pouch so heavy with diamonds that the bird was unable to take off.

So tough is security that since 1927 no vehicle or machine has ever left the Oranjemund Diamond Mine. In fact, a vast dump — the disused equipment park — contains row upon row of lorries, trucks, bulldozers, cranes, some of the largest earth-moving equipment ever built, and acres of old tyres, all spread out over kilometres of barren landscape.

Almost 100 per cent of the stones are of gem quality, mainly colourless or pale yellow. Namibia's 'fancy' diamonds, infrequently found, are varied in colour, often pink, and unequalled for quality.

CDM is Namibia's major taxpayer, contributing between sixty and sixty-four per cent of its profits to the national exchequer. Indeed, in 1981 it accounted for ninety-seven per cent of all tax revenue.

Production remains strictly controlled. CDM is a subsidiary of the South African De Beers conglomerate run by the Oppenheimer dynasty. When over-production threatened prices, the family closed down most of the Namibian mines — the world's sixth-largest producer — and they continue to maintain control of the market. Although in the 1990s, when world markets were flooded by cut-price diamonds from the former Soviet Union, and illicitly-mined stones from Angola, the traditional structure was close to collapse.

Consolidated Diamond Mines was also angered when an American entrepreneur was given a concession to mine diamonds between the high and low tidemarks along the forbidden coast. While they initiated legal action, the American put a fleet of costly dredging barges to work sucking gravel from the sea-bed. In the end CDM took over the operation but the potential for offshore diamonds has never been really viable.

All the way along the forbidden coast, a string of curiously named islands — stretching north beyond Lüderitz — underlined the strange anomaly of South Africa's continued role in independent Namibia, even as late as 1993. For if Roast Beef and Black Rock islands were part of the country's sovereignty, others such as Plum Pudding, Sinclair's, Pomona, Albatross, Possession, South Long, North Long, Halifax, Penguin, Seal, Ichaboe and Mercury islands remained marked on the map as South African territory — with no word to explain why one should be different from the other.

But there is much more to Namibia than deserts and diamonds. The dried-up course of another once mighty river of the south lingers in the mind when most other memories have faded. West of the 2,134-metre Karas Mountains, and the first stretch of highway between Noordoewer and Grünau, a winding trail leads

Above: Namibia's abundance of diamonds is almost unequalled. Some say that when it rains the ground glistens with precious stones.

Following Pages: Green oases mark the dry river bed of the mighty Fish River Canyon some 536 metres beneath the rugged cliffs that cut 160 kilometres through the wastelands of southern Namibia.

through a bleached wasteland to one of Africa's great natural wonders. During thousands of years, the Fish River has cut a 536-metre-deep chasm in the rocky, barren plains that is twenty-seven kilometres across at its widest. Twisting 160 kilometres through eroded cliffs, staggering in their rugged beauty, the Fish River Canyon is one of the earth's greatest canyons. One road runs along the edge of the canyon to a series of viewing points where sheer cliffs plunge to the river bed which is a billion years old.

In an area often plagued by drought, the well-watered canyon, with its fish and game, was an oasis for early inhabitants. By 1981 more than forty Stone Age sites had been recorded, increasing in size where the canyon begins to widen in the south. Fish River Canyon was proclaimed a national monument in 1962, became a game reserve in 1968 and a conservation area in 1969. The reserve was expanded in 1987 to include the Huns Mountains to the west and land to the south.

Centrepiece of the canyon, which began forming about 500 million years ago, is a ninety-kilometre nature trail, involving a four- to five-day hike. From the main lookout, the trail leads down into the canyon and Hell's Bend — a classic example of a meander which originated when the river was young. Recently a second hiking trail in the canyon, the Fish Eagle Hiking Trail, was opened. This trail in the upper part of the canyon is undertaken with a guide.

The longest river in Namibia, the Fish River, flows more than 800 kilometres to its confluence with the Orange River, 110 kilometres east of the Atlantic. Some kilometres south of the Gaab River, which is where the Fish Eagle Trail begins, it plunges over two waterfalls and enters the canyon. Its flow varies with the rains, usually between November and March. But it is the only Namibian river that has permanent pools outside the rainy season. In spate it becomes a raging 91-metre-wide torrent tearing through the gorge at up to twenty-five kilometres an hour. In 1972 it destroyed a newly-built rest camp, except for the main building on the high ground.

The strata of the cliffs were initially sandstone, shale and lava deposited almost two billion years ago. Five hundred million years later they folded over and, compressed deep in the earth's surface, heated up to more than 600°C. This caused metamorphosis, re-crystallising the rock and changing its appearance. The dark lines which cut the canyon walls are fractures filled with lava that never reached the surface.

When the first major erosion began some 850 million years ago, it exposed the rock strata and levelled them into a vast peneplain — becoming the bed of a shallow sea — that covered southern Namibia. Five hundred million years ago the crust fractured, forming a north-south valley, which was deepened 200 million years later by Ice Age glaciers. The uplifting of the sedimentary strata in the area increased erosion caused by the river, as the glaciers began to melt, so

that the gorge became deeper still. The fractures are clearly visible five kilometres along the nature trail.

Above: Safari bus perches at a vantage point over the incomparable Fish River Canyon.

Hobas, an overnight camping site, is ten kilometres from the main lookout and descent point into the canyon. After slithering down, clutching hold of the chains that slow the descent on the steeper sections, there is much to see on the valley floor. The trail leads to the palm-shaded Sulphur Springs, fifteen kilometres south. Other trees and shrubs that flourish in the valley's winter temperatures of 20-25°C include tamarisk, camel-thorn, ringwood, buffalo thorn, wild fig, ebony, euphorbia, sweet thorn and the green-hair tree.

Klipspringer, their thick, bushy coats protecting them from falls, their hooves adapted for rock climbing, haunt the canyon which is, for them, an ideal habitat, along with kudu, the nocturnal Hartmann's mountain zebra, rock dassie, ground squirrel and chacma baboon. These are stalked by leopard. Ostrich also live in the canyon where the cliffs and pools echo to the call of the purple

Above: Delicate beauty of flowering desert cactus.

gallinule, marsh warbler, white-backed mousebird, red-eyed bulbul, blacksmith plover, hammerkop, Egyptian goose, grey heron, Cape robin, rock kestrel, rock pigeon, chats, starlings and dusky sunbird.

Alternately seeking shade and heat to control their body temperature, cold-blooded reptiles, including three species of deadly African adder and the Egyptian cobra, survive among the rocks and shrubs. The canyon's perennial pools sustain good numbers of barbel and yellow-fish, providing ideal sport for the angler.

The impressive Four Finger Rock dominates the halfway stage of the trail and, just beyond, is the grave of a German officer killed by the Nama in 1905. From there it is a good day's walk to the hot springs of Ai-Ais, a vernacular word meaning Fire Water, once the home of Neolithic man. During the Nama rebellion in the first decade of this century the Germans made it their base. The 60°C waters, a mixture of fluoride, sulphate and chloride, are fed to an outdoor swimming pool and jacuzzis. Today it is a popular spa resort. From there, the Fish River winds away — through a ravaged range of forbidding and uninhabited mountains — to join the Orange River in the south.

The rest camp at Ai-Ais is open from the second Friday in March until 31 October, and hikes in the canyon are from the beginning of May until the end of September.

Gazing down into the canyon from the deep, precipitous cliffs, the words of Samuel Taylor Coleridge in his famous 1816 poem *Kubla Khan* come to mind:

In Xanadu did Kubla Khan
A stately pleasure-dome decree;
Where Alph, the sacred river, ran
Through caverns measureless to man
Down to a sunless sea . . .
But oh! that deep romantic chasm which slanted
Down the green hill athwart a cedarn cover!
A savage place! as holy and enchanted
As e'er beneath a waning moon was haunted
By woman wailing for her demon-lover!

Back on the main highway, Keetmanshoop forms a junction between Lüderitz and the Namib in the west, with Windhoek in the north, and the Kalahari in the east. Namibia's fourth-largest town, on the banks of the seasonal Swartmodder River, is a thriving centre founded on the site of an 1866 mission station. Linked by rail to the port of Lüderitz, Keetmanshoop became the gateway to the interior and prospered from the wealth of the southern diamond fields early this century. Wealthy prospectors could afford European luxuries, and the shops of Keetmanshoop were filled with the treasures of Paris, Berlin and London.

Others established farms or squandered their fortunes on high living and the gaming tables. The town's wide streets are lined with some superb examples of colonial architecture, notably the stone church and old post office which is now a museum. The mission station and school, both of which are still in use today, were built by the Reverend Thomas Fenchel who served in Keetmanshoop from 1877 to 1910.

During a flash flood in October 1890, the missionary and his family had to be rescued when their house was flooded and the church swept away. The pulpit and bible were recovered from the flood and have been preserved in the new church which the preacher built. It had room for 1,000 worshippers and served all races in Keetmanshoop until 1930. Recently the church, notable for its hand-carved woodwork, was restored. The town is named after Johann Keetman, a wealthy German industrialist and chairman of the Rhenish Missionary Society.

To the east of the town, on the road to Koës, grows the eerie Quiver Tree Forest, one of Namibia's great natural curiosities. The forest's 300 kokerboom trees, *Aloe dichotoma,* spread out some distance from each other, cover the rust-coloured slopes with a supernatural look. Like the Namib's *Welwitschia mirabilis,* the kokerboom, also known as the quiver tree, has had to adapt to its barren, inhospitable environment. Growing as high as seven metres, the fibrous trunk, spindly branches and pithy leaves develop into water containers — their slow growth and waxy surface coating help the trees withstand the arid climate. In the depth of the southern winter, during June and July, the radiant yellow flowers at the top of the plants burst into bloom, bringing the bronzed landscape to life. The San use the fibrous core of the hollowed-out branches as pincushion-like quivers for their arrows. Close by the Quiver Tree Forest is the Giant's Playground, an unusual formation of volcanic rocks, weathered over millions of years.

Above: Red flowering succulent in private garden, Keetmanshoop.

Spread across 130 square kilometres, the Gellap Ost Karakul Farm, also near the Quiver Tree Forest, was founded as a sheep breeding centre by Paul Albert Thorer. He imported a flock of karakul sheep, a hardy central Asian breed, into Namibia in 1907. The Namibian-bred sheepskins are regarded as the finest in the world — and include pure white karakul pelts, found nowhere else. They are taken from lambs slaughtered twenty-four hours after birth.

More than 250 kilometres east of Keetmanshoop, on the Sandheuwel Game Ranch, deep in the Kalahari Desert, more than fifty species of mammals — including the Kalahari lion — are visible from the luxury of the Kalahari Game Lodge. With game drives and walks, horse-trekking and hot-air balloon safaris, the sanctuary is an oasis of delight for nature lovers.

Keetmanshoop is the turnoff for the intriguing run west through the Namib diamond fields to the fairy-tale town of Lüderitz. Twice a year, at Easter and in July, Namibian Railways celebrates the pioneering days of steam. A Diamond

Above: Balancing rocks at The Giant's Playground near Keetmanshoop in southern Namibia silhouetted against the setting sun.

Train, hauled by a majestic Class 24 locomotive, steams the 334 kilometres from Keetmanshoop to Lüderitz. When the journey begins, a cloud of white doves are released in the bright blue Namibian sky as the train passes under a ceremonial arch at Keetmanshoop station. Aboard the train, 200 passengers are entertained by a band, which plays a Diamond Train Song composed by Crispin Clay, the bard of Lüderitz. The dining and lounge cars are decked out in the livery of the early days of the diamond rush.

About 100 or so kilometres from Keetmanshoop on the road to Lüderitz, a spur leads thirty kilometres north to the small town of Bethanie. Its old London Missionary Society station, the first in Namibia, was founded by a German missionary, the Reverend Heinrich Schmelen. He had vowed to preach the word to the Hottentot Khoikhoi who had migrated there, but he abandoned the station in 1822 after war broke out between the Nama and the Herero. One relic of his time survives. *Schmelenhaus*, Schmelen's simple one-story cottage, built in

Opposite: Tawny grassland slopes of the Auas Mountains which ring Windhoek.

Above: Spare-framed survivors of the mean desert — Africa's only herd of wild desert horses have adapted for survival in the arid plains of the southern Namib.

1814, and then rebuilt after it was burnt down — is the oldest European building in Namibia. Another national monument is the house of Joseph Fredericks, the nineteenth-century Hottentot chief. It was there that the first treaty between the Germans and the Hottentots was signed.

One of nature's great surprises, Africa's only herd of desert horses, roams the Namib west of Aus, a small town midway between Keetmanshoop and Lüderitz. As the chestnut steeds wander the sandflats, they seem like a mirage. The hardy creatures have adapted to life in a thirsty land. Conserving their energy they can exist five days without water, for the only source these creatures have is the artificial pan at Garub which is supplied from a borehole. The herd remains one of the great riddles of the Namib and no one is certain how they came to live in the hostile desert. One theory is that they are descendants of horses left behind when the German garrison abandoned their base at Aus in 1915.

Above: These massive cubes of golden stone near Keetmanshoop are nicknamed The Giant's Playground.

Constantly cloaked in the grey silt of the desert, Aus is reminiscent of a ghost town. And, in a sense, it is one — for it was there that German NCOs, and other ranks, were interned in 1915 as POWs in a hastily built camp of tents. These were so unsuitable that the Germans built themselves permanent blocks using mud-baked bricks, tiled with flattened tin cans, while their guards remained in primitive shanties made of hessian. The ruins of the old POW houses are still visible.

A picnic site situated midway between Aus and Lüderitz in the shade of a rare clump of trees at the side of the road, offers excellent views of distant mountains. There, where the relentless winds force the dunes ever forward, a constant battle is maintained to prevent the desert from burying the road and railway. The great sand dunes threaten to obliterate them, and would do so if it were not for the bulldozers stationed to hold the Namib, the oldest wilderness on earth, at bay.

The desert's complex and fragile ecosystem, evolved over thirty million years, is one of the world's most fascinating natural regions, with dramatic 300-metre mountains of sand at Sossusvlei. The Namib runs the entire 1,600-kilometre length of Namibia's seaboard in a band ranging between 150 and 200 kilometres wide, extending from Angola in the north; to south of the Orange River in South Africa; and eastwards to Namibia's central escarpment.

The Atlantic's mysterious Benguela Current, born in the Antarctic, creates the climate that gives tenuous life to the Namib, providing moisture for a wealth of rare and hardy plants and creatures.

It consists of a permanent anticyclone which forces southerly winds north-

Above: The Naute Dam on the Löwen River, south-east of Keetmanshoop, holds over 80 million cubic metres of water. The magnificent surroundings make it one of the country's most popular watersports and angling resorts.

west along the coast. This remarkably stable weather system serves to lower overall temperatures along the coast, influencing the flow of the slow surface current — that causes an unusually cold upwelling from the 300-metre depths of the Atlantic.

Although the nutrient-rich waters support prolific sea life — a great many microscopic marine plants and sea creatures, as well as the larger species that feed upon them — there is a more important consequence. The convergence of cold and warm water with the air temperatures that prevail at this latitude, creates dense fogs. These sweep far inland over the Namib for at least 100 days a year. The desert plants and creatures survive by drawing moisture from the mist. The fog covers all — plants, rocks and creatures — leaving them coated in condensation.

What there is of the Namib's annual rainfall varies from region to region. Its western flank, on the Atlantic, usually receives about fifteen millimetres a year; while in the east, the Namib enjoys as much as 100 millimetres. The Namib is at its driest in the central region. Rainfall, however, is always erratic and occasionally the Namib is swamped by uncharacteristic downpours, rare and heavy enough to be remembered vividly, such as those in 1934 and 1976. But there are many years when no rain falls at all.

Wind and sun, as well as fog, also shape the Namib, adding to its character. Prevailing winds carry detritus, tiny pieces of organic material, to its innermost reaches, providing nourishment for creatures far from vegetation. Hills of sand characterize the Namib — star dunes, parabolic dunes, barchan dunes and sief dunes — each sculpted in their individual way. Each dune is home to a wide

Above: Typical wildlife design distinguishes Namibia's handwoven carpets.

Opposite top: Namibian woolsmith weaves a tapestry of pastoral Namibia from karakul wool.

Opposite: Bundles of brightly-coloured karakul wool hung out to dry in the heat of the afternoon after being dyed.

variety of creatures from tiny insects to the largest lizard. The slipface — shifting sand — on the crest hosts more life than the rest of one of these massive sandhills.

Of all the dunes, the most mobile are the extraordinary barchan dunes which move between two and three metres each year. Shaped by strong winds, blowing in a north-easterly direction, these crescent-shaped mountains of sand roll along, taking their residents with them. With the prevailing winds blowing from the south, the Namib's dunes are forever roaming northwards — their movement only ceasing when they come to a river bed. Dried up or in spate, these rivers are formidable barriers whose influence helps to shape this living desert. They also play a profound role in the character of the ecosystem for they limit the movement of the creatures living within the dune, narrowing their range of options in the struggle for survival. Millennia of desert evolution have equipped every creature with an armoury of techniques by which to stay alive. The most important of these survival methods is the ability to create micro-habitats. Through these it is possible to escape the desert's vicious conditions almost entirely. Indeed, the blind golden mole, found only in the Namib's sand dunes, burrows down sixty centimetres during the day to evade the scorching surface temperatures. It reappears to begin its nocturnal prowl for beetles, crickets and small geckos only after sundown. Lizards, such as the shovel-snouted lizard, endure the blistering heat of the slipface by alternately raising each leg in a foot-lifting 'thermal' dance, allowing the foot to cool. They scuttle across the sands, ready to dive deep beneath the surface at the first hostile footfall. Indeed, many desert dwellers escape the unbearable heat by tunnelling

Above: Built in 1895, Keetmanshoop's church was used until 1930. It was designated a national monument in 1978, and is now used as the town's museum.

under the sand. Although they move about the slipfaces during the day, tenebrionid beetles also dive beneath the sand when it is too hot. But at night, or early in the morning, they give an insight into their secrets for survival with a glimpse of one of the marvels of this barren wilderness — 'fog-basking'. The black beetles are masters at tapping the roaming desert mists to slake their thirst.

As the chill fog billows inland, the tiny insects resurface and turn their bodies into the icy wind, extending their rear legs while standing on their heads. In moments, the back of the beetle grows wet and droplets of condensation slide down their chests into their mouths. So precious is this moisture that in a single session the beetles guzzle up to forty per cent of their body weight in water.

Most plains animals find the dunes difficult to negotiate and prefer life on the open desert plains where there is more vegetation. They do, however, often venture into the dunes in search of sparse grazing. And their ability to tolerate

Above: Ripening vines in a rare, green corner of southern Namibia near Keetmanshoop, mark the first stage of a vintage Namibian wine.

extreme temperatures is fascinating. Larger creatures, such as the ostrich, springbok and oryx, position their body to place the smallest possible area in direct sunlight. In particular, the gemsbok has made an art of desert survival. It always finds high points with the strongest breeze and, although warm-blooded, has the ability when dehydrated and unable to sweat, to raise its body temperature to levels fatal to other mammals. It can sustain temperatures of up to 45°C for about eight hours. Most mammals die when their body temperature is above 42°C. The key to the gemsbok's success seems to be its ability to keep its brain cooler than the rest of its body — three degrees lower — due to a complex network of blood vessels beneath its skull; and an extraordinary evaporation system in the nose that cools the blood as it enters the brain.

The survival techniques of the Namib creatures are endless. Ground squirrels raise their tails as sunshades. Ants crawl up tiny stems of grass for shade. Meerkats make complex underground burrows. And the male sandgrouse is

Opposite: Formerly the thriving home of diamond miners, Kolmanskop is now a ghost town where the insidious Namib desert has taken up residence in the once-elegant mansions.

Above: Functional tower of the church at Aus is a fine example of rustic colonial architecture.

able to retain water within its breast feathers, allowing it to fly long distances to and from its ground nest to quench the thirst of its chicks.

No less amazing is the Namib's plant life. No matter how long they remain dormant, the seeds of many Namib plants are able to withstand the extreme cold or heat. Consequently, germination is swift. On average, no plant takes more than about three weeks to flower and bear seed. As if by magic, after a few moments of steady rain, the landscape turns into a thriving profusion of colourful plants and grasses, desperately trying to flourish and regenerate before the remorseless drought returns. Many are succulents that have evolved to store large quantities of water in the trunk, leaves, roots or stems. Their cells have developed the capacity to stretch and hoard extra supplies. Most succulents carry their photosynthetic cells in their stems or trunk and have few leaves, if any, thus limiting evaporation.

The diamond fever that swept southern Namibia early this century began at a

Above: Once one of the finest buildings in southern Africa, this Kolmanskop mansion now lies forgotten and forlorn.

place in the Namib called Kolmanskop which is near Grasplatz, a small railway station 300 kilometres west of Keetmanshoop. Kolmanskop took its name from one of the first visitors to the desolate region, Jani Kolman, who had to be rescued when a voortrek of ox-wagons he was leading from Lüderitz to Keetmanshoop was overwhelmed by a sandstorm. Much later Kolmanskop became a boom town — mushrooming from a single shack to a bustling community in months — after Zacharias Lewala's diamond discovery in April 1908.

Lewala gave the stone to August Stauch and, within days, he and other prospectors had pegged claims covering almost the whole coast from Conception Bay in the north to Marmora in the south.

The diamond was no freak find but proof of the immense riches that this seemingly barren land had to offer. In fact, the southern Namib was one vast diamond field — a fact spectacularly confirmed one night when Stauch and Professor R. Scheibe, a geologist, visited Edatal, one of the valleys in the dunes. The desert winds had laid bare gravels so rich in diamonds that workmen dropped their loads and scooped them up by their hands. Soon there were so many that the men, not knowing where to put them, began stuffing them into their mouths. One observer recalled that the diamonds lay glistening on the desert floor by the light of a full moon 'like plums under a plum tree'.

Before a year had passed, prospectors were clawing away the desert sands at such remote places as Kolmanskop, Stauchslager, Charlottental and Bogenfels. And a year later Elisabethbucht had joined the diamond rush, followed in 1912 by Pomona. Settlements spread across the desert and, as thousands flocked in to

Above: Abandoned and crumbling ruins of a house at Kolmanskop, near Lüderitz, where Namibia's diamond industry was born.

search for riches, Stauch became a millionaire playing a major role in developing South West Africa's livestock industry. But when he died in near penury in Germany on 6 May, 1947 he left behind him in Africa a fortune close to a million pounds.

At the time, however, the De Beers diamond conglomerate predicted that the Kolmanskop pipe would never be worth more than a million and a half carats. In fact, the sands of Kolmanskop produced enormous wealth. Shops and houses rose up overnight along with other enterprises designed to cash in on the riches being dug out of the ground. In its heyday, Kolmanskop was said to be more European than Europe.

With their new-found wealth the inhabitants were able to afford all the luxuries and sophistication of a great city. There was a soft drink bottling plant, swimming pool, skittle alley — even a theatre with orchestra. The mining manager and engineers lived in elegant houses with fine, arched windows, balconies and verandahs, overlooking the vastness of the desert. Soon, roads and pipelines linked Kolmanskop to Lüderitz and other parts of German South West Africa.

One major problem was establishing sufficient supplies of fresh water. A borehole in the desert, 100 kilometres away at Garub, brought some relief. But most water was shipped in by sea from Cape Town to Lüderitz and hauled to Kolmanskop by mule. It was too costly to use in the diamond mine, however, so sea water was pumped thirty-five kilometres from Elizabeth Bay on the coast to the processing plant. Some was also turned into drinking water by a primitive prototype distillation plant, forerunner of today's desalination systems.

Previous Pages: Lüderitz, once a remote anchorage on the hostile African coastline, today teems with activity.

Kolmanskop's star began to wane in the years after the Great War with the worldwide slump in diamond sales. It was also hard hit by the discovery of the staggeringly rich diamond fields at Oranjemund. These reasons, coupled to the fact that the diamond seams were running dry, meant that Kolmanskop slowly died. By 1956 just one resident remained, and the desert had stolen back what hordes of rapacious prospectors had come to plunder. Other similar diamond ghost towns in the desert are Pomona, Bogenfels, Elisabethbucht and Charlottental. There, among the sands, stand macabre relics of immense riches — broken wheelbarrows and desolate graveyards where the wind and sand have rubbed away the names of the dead, and where, in the shimmering whiteness of a salt pan, shrubs struggle for existence.

The glory of Kolmanskop's grand architecture has all but vanished beneath the desert sands. Some buildings, such as the old casino, have been partially restored by CDM, creating an open-air museum. Indeed, one shop which counted August Stauch among its customers, in what was once described as 'The Pearl of the Desert', now hosts a display of historical photographs and memorabilia of its grand days. But no more does the town echo to the rumble of mining machines, or the solemn hum of the town's ice factory. The butchery and bakery, the school and the skittle alley, even a wine cellar, have been drowned in a sea of sand.

The hospital, once proud of its X-ray machine — the first in Africa — lies like a giant tomb. Kolmanskop is now a ghost town where the only voice is that of the wind, moaning through the crumbling remains of shacks and houses. And as it whistles in and out of the empty window frames, it seems to murmur Shelley's lines in disdain of mankind.

'My name is Ozymandias, king of kings:
Look on my works, ye Mighty and despair!'
Nothing beside remains. Round the decay
Of that colossal wreck, boundless and bare
The lone and level sands stretch far away.

As the area is still in a diamond concession, a permit is needed to visit Kolmanskop. These are given out for a small fee at the mine offices in Lüderitz, nine kilometres away.

Lüderitz, the largest town on Namibia's southern coast, was declared a municipality in 1909. But its history goes back long before diamonds were discovered — to the days of Bartholomeo Diaz who first moored there in 1488. He was taking refuge from the Atlantic swell — and the barren emptiness of the Namib, which he called the Sands of Hell. Diaz, the first European known to have ventured so far along the south-west coast of Africa, planted a stone cross on a rocky promontory looking out across the seascape. But, despondent at the

Above: Lüderitz is famous for its magnificent Imperial German and art nouveau styles of architecture.

idea that the barren shore would never end, he abandoned his search for a new route to India and returned to Portugal.

Then, as now, the sheltered harbour was a welcome and congenial contrast to the pounding surf of the Namibian coast. But, although a safe haven from the Atlantic's stormy seas, Lüderitz was as devoid of drinking water as the rest of the Namib. Nonetheless, whaling vessels, and those mining the nitrogen-rich guano deposits, continued to use its natural harbour.

It was in 1883 that Heinrich Vogelsang, an agent of the Bremen trader and tobacco dealer, Adolf Lüderitz, bought the bay from Joseph Fredericks, chief of the Bethanie Khoikhoi people. Soon after, Lüderitz made another audacious investment, staggering in its presumption, when he snapped up the entire coastline between *Angra Pequena* and the Orange River — together with its thirty-two-kilometre wide inland littoral — from Fredericks, who claimed he owned the land. Lüderitz, who arrived to inspect his investment in October of

Above: One of many outstanding architectural treasures built early this century on solid bedrock on the heights above Lüderitz Harbour.

the same year, hoped the desert concealed mineral treasures that would make him rich. But he never found out, for soon afterwards he disappeared mysteriously while sailing from the Orange River to Lüderitz Bay in a small boat.

Lüderitz remained modest in size until the diamond boom shaped it into a charming and magnificent town, its distinctive architecture giving it the ambience of a little Germany, a teutonic outpost far from its European homeland. Although it no longer enjoys the hustle and bustle of the glorious days of old, this fishing town of 5,000 people does have a stately enchantment, its mellow buildings slumbering in a mantle of antiquity.

The town and fishing port lie on the sheltered side of a deep inlet where Shark Island, linked to the mainland by a causeway, has created Robert Harbour. A bronze plaque attached to a rock on Shark Island honours the town's founder, Adolf Lüderitz. To the west, across the inlet which forms the natural harbour of Lüderitz, is Griffith Bay, named after an American fugitive from the civil war who was executed for desertion when discovered by the captain of a visiting American ship. It is on a rocky peninsula that ends at Angra Point, the eastern side of the great sweep of north-facing Shearwater Bay. Diaz Point stands on the bay's western arm, overlooking Guano Bay and Halifax Island.

Characterised by clear blue skies with occasional gales, mist and rain, Lüderitz rejoices in long periods of sunny days. The temperate climate encourages swimming in its sheltered bays while the bracing waters of the nutrient-rich Benguela Current sustain the port's fishing industry. The coast

Above: The new wealth of Lüderitz — a mouthwatering selection of crayfish, part of the harvest from the sea which revived the town's fortunes after the collapse of the Kolmanskop diamond boom.

yields a rich harvest of anchovy, pilchard and crayfish. Other creatures of the sea and shore feed off this abundance. These waters are also the basis of a major rock lobster industry. Frozen lobsters are exported to Japan, while the USA imports frozen tails. But fishing for crustacea is only allowed between November and April.

All along this craggy coast, the crystal-clear shallows reveal many wonders of the deep — shellfish and sea anemones and a diversity of marine plants on the rocky sea-bed — while holiday makers go surfing or surf fishing.

While over the tempestuous sea gannets swoop down to catch fish, inland marvellous plants with strange names — such as *Crassulae* and *Lithops*, known as 'living stones'— flourish in the desert: a slice of which has been turned into an improbably green golf course, echoes of more prosperous days.

During the Herero and Nama uprising between 1904 and 1907 German forces called for an extension of the harbour and a railway into the interior. In 1907, the Woermann Line, which shipped troops and ammunition to South West Africa, built Woermann House, an enormous headquarters with offices and living quarters, that still stands.

Soon planning regulations outlawed the crude tin shacks which until then had dominated the town. A magistrate ruled that 'corrugated iron houses do not offer sufficient protection against wind and sand, are swelteringly hot in summer and do not last'.

Within the next ten years, spurred by the wealth of the diamond boom, Lüderitz developed into the town known today — rich in its architectural character. Paradoxically, the slump which followed the closure of the

Above: Springbok take flight along the Atlantic coast of Lüderitz Bay.

Kolmanskop diamond fields — relieved only by the development of a rock lobster industry — helped preserve the town's heritage. For, if development had continued at the same pace, many of the early buildings in Lüderitz would have been demolished to make way for new developments.

In this improbable setting, an enclave of civilisation between the sea of sand and the deep waters of the Atlantic, the architectural combination of art nouveau and German imperial styles give the town a Gothic fairy-tale ambience.

The most imposing edifice is the railway station, completed in 1914, seven years after the railway line between Lüderitz and Aus — 125 kilometres to the east — was laid. In those days the station was the centre of town life — passengers waiting in its hall before the trip eastwards to the interior. Eventually the line was linked up with the whole of German South West Africa.

Two architect brothers, Heinrich and Albert Bause, contributed to much of Lüderitz's grandeur. Among the buildings they designed is the Deutsche-

Afrika-Bank, completed in 1907, with a Renaissance-style bell tower and gable, which testifies to their talents. But their most exceptional achievement is the Evangelical Lutheran 'Church on the Rocks' — *Felsenkirche* — at the southern end of the town, looking out over a motley collection of rooftops to the harbour beyond. Albert Bause designed the church, which was completed in 1912, while his brother was responsible for the parsonage.

The church is in complete contrast to many of Lüderitz's neo-Gothic imperial buildings and seems to have been influenced by those in Cape Town where the brothers once lived. It was paid for by public subscriptions from Germany and Kaiser Wilhelm II donated the altar window and the spectacular stained-glass windows — bearing his name and the imperial eagle of Germany — while his wife presented the altar bible. On its crude stone base, and with its stone tower, the church looks as if it has been hewn from the surrounding rock.

The most spectacular of all Lüderitz's buildings is *Goerke House* on Diamond Hill. Seen from the streets of the town below, the house with its snaking stairway looks more like a fortress than the home. There a businessman, Hans Goerke, lived in the lap of colonial luxury for three years between 1909 and 1912. His home, which boasts a unique *Wilheminische* sundial on its facade, was acquired by Consolidated Diamond Mines in 1920 — and taken over as a magistrate's residency by the South West Africa Administration in 1944. When it was no longer needed for this purpose, CDM bought it back.

With its tangled lanes and jumbled red and white rooftops, Lüderitz is deceptively beguiling for both traveller and resident. The empty wastes of the nearby desert and ocean seem far away. But walk up to Nautilus Hill which overlooks the town and there are splendid views of both.

And from the harbour it is possible to take a yacht to Diaz Point, where the navigator is commemorated by a marble replica of his cross. Remnants of the original cross are displayed in museums in Windhoek, Cape Town and Lisbon. On nearby Halifax Island, off the sweltering African coast, a creature forever associated with the Antarctic ice has made its home — the penguin. And on this and other islands, and in the coastal lagoons, a pale, pink blush of flamingo is ever present.

3·

FINGER OF GOD, SEA OF SAND

Previous Pages: Awesome expanses of the Namib, the world's oldest desert, stretch away in an unending horizon of sand mountains.

Nature moulded Great Namaqualand in unusual fashion. Southern Namibia is an arid region where less than 200 millimetres of rain falls each year, but the seemingly endless barren plains are interspersed by batholiths which have been uncovered by erosion — such as the Karasberge and the Hunsberge, which give it dramatic shape and form. One such mountain, the Brukkarros, dominates the western horizon on the drive from Keetmanshoop to Mariental. Its volcano-like shape was caused when the upliftment — due to underground pressure — was exposed by erosion. The tiring thirty-minute walk to its rim is rewarded with a stupendous view over the surrounding countryside.

In the 1930s, Washington's Smithsonian Institute built an observatory on the western rim to study the sun. Earlier, the Germans built a heliograph signalling station, still there on the opposite crest.

The eastern sector of Namibia is occupied by the Kalahari. Long before mankind trekked across its measureless wastes, a single 33-metre column of rock looked down on the western flank of the great desert. For millennium after millennium this Finger of God, *Mukurob*, midway between Keetmanshoop and Mariental on the major Namibian highway in the centre of Great Nama Land, bore witness to the extraordinary forces that eroded the great Weissrand Plateau. It resembled a giant totem pole carved out of rock. But it is no more. The towering 637-tonne obelisk toppled during a windstorm on 8 December 1988. Some say that the earthquake in Armenia, which took place at the time of the fall, could have been the cause. Tremors from that earthquake were felt in southern Africa. Whatever the reason, the Finger of God was reduced to rubble.

Above: Employee and young resident at an ostrich farm in Mariental

North of Asab, where this dramatic natural obelisk stood, is Gibeon, which is little more than a railway station. The small graveyard nearby, however, testifies to one of the bloodiest battles of World War I in South West Africa. Fifteen hundred South African troops — under Brigadier-General Sir Duncan McKenzie — and a German force of 800 — commanded by General von Kleist — met on 27 April 1915. When the fighting ended, twenty-nine South Africans lay dead along with twelve Germans, while the Allies suffered sixty-six wounded to the Germans' thirty. The South Africans took another 188 prisoner and captured a trainload of arms and ammunition.

The area was also at the centre of one of the world's largest meteorite showers, scattered over 20,000 square kilometres. Seventy-seven fragments, weighing a total of twenty-one tonnes have been collected since 1911, some of which are on display at Windhoek's Meteor Fountain in the centre of town. The largest fragment, weighing 650 kilos, however, is now in a Cape Town museum.

Gochas, several kilometres east of Gibeon, was the site of an old German fort built in 1897 which has since disappeared. But in the cemetery near the post office, the graves of many soldiers killed in battle against the Nama still survive. The land between Gochas and Stampriet is an important fruit and vegetable growing region.

Above: Ostrich chicks reared at Mariental.

But even when bursting with colourful blossoms there are constant reminders of the 1904-1907 uprisings. From Stampriet it is a comfortable ride to Mariental, with its many petrol stations, information centre and striking Dutch Reformed Church — the foundation stone of which was laid in September, 1920.

Twenty-four kilometres north-west of the town, at the edge of the wilderness, stands Hardap Dam. Popular with watersports enthusiasts, the placid surface of the twenty-five-square-kilometre lake formed by the dam is also an avian paradise. Osprey, flamingo, fish eagle, pelican and goliath heron trawl its shores and surface. Barbel, carp, mud mullet, small-mouth yellowfish and blue kurper make the lake a magnet for anglers as well as birds. The dam is also used as a breeding centre for freshwater fish. It was planned to tap the hydroelectric potential of the Great Fish River at the end of last century but work on the 39-metre-deep dam did not start until 1960. When full, more than four million litres a second pour down the dam's four spillways. The lake's western shores form the wildlands of the Hardap Game

Reserve where, as the azure waters mirror the tropic sky, ostrich, kudu, eland, cheetah, gemsbok and zebra find afternoon shade among the scattered low-lying acacia.

The small village of Maltahöhe lies 135 kilometres west of Mariental where a junction leads eighty kilometres south to one of the great anachronisms of southern Africa — the magnificent, castellated sandstone fortress of *Schloss Duwisib*. It was built on the edge of the Namib sands in 1908 by a German aristocrat, Baron Hans-Heinrich von Wolf, after he had completed his service as an army captain in South West Africa. The Baron, who went home to Dresden in 1907 and married Jayta Humphries, the American Consul's stepdaughter, then returned with her to build the *schloss* and establish a series of enormous farms in the region. Craftsmen from Italy, Ireland, Denmark and Sweden were shipped in to build the twenty-two room fortress. The gregarious Baron's main interest was his stud farm. Once the castle was complete, the fixtures and fittings, including antique furniture, weapons and portraits from the seventeenth and eighteenth centuries, were ferried ashore from a ship anchored off the Namib. Then they were hauled across the desert by hand. In 1914, the couple sailed for England to buy stallions for their stud farm. When World War I broke out their boat was diverted to South America where they were interned. The Baron, however, talked them aboard a neutral ship which carried them to Germany where he re-enlisted as a captain. He was killed in the 1916 battle of the Somme and his widow never returned to their castle. She lived out her life in Munich, moving to Switzerland during World War II. Even now, the castle stands alone in the wilderness at the edge of the Namib.

Above: World's largest bird, the ostrich, patrols the dry bed of one of the Namib's seasonal rivers where the roots of thorn trees tap down into subterranean water reserves.

From the castle, the desert trail swings 139 kilometres north-west to Sesriem and Namib-Naukluft Park, Africa's largest, and the world's fourth largest conservation area. Bigger than Switzerland, the park's 49,000 square kilometres, spread between southern and central Namibia, are an extraordinary geological treasure. Granite mountains, gypsum and quartz plains, sand dunes and canyons and estuarine lagoons, were joined together in 1978 by the merger of the Namib Desert Park and the Naukluft Mountain Zebra Park. Large areas of unoccupied state land, together with old diamond concessions, were also included. The broad band of the park, which reaches north as far as Walvis Bay and Swakopmund, contains many different ecosystems, each complementing the other.

The southern reaches of the park are dominated by the dramatic cliffs and deep ravines which form the plateau of the 2,276-metre Naukluft Mountains. At the bottom of some of these ravines, translucent springs and pools are framed by fascinating formations of soft limestone — left behind aeons ago by the waterfalls which once gushed there. The abundance of water in this arid land made Naukluft an obvious refuge for early and Stone Age man. He left rock pictures of the wildlife and the community's lifestyle. Ancient game traps have been uncovered and also crude ladders — sticks hammered into a cliff face to reach the beehives above. In

Above: Flowering in December, the Kalahari Christmas tree or Sickle tree.

the last century the mountains were a fortress for the Khoikhoi who fought bloody hit-and-run battles with the Germans.

The range, the western edge of Namibia's great inland plateau, is composed mainly of dolomite and limestone which has been riven in many places by seasonal streams and downpours giving rise to an extensive underground drainage system.

These barren mountains are now preserved as one of the world's great unspoilt wildernesses where backpackers can take an eight-day trek along a splendid nature trail that switchbacks up and down between 1,372 and 1,951 metres. There is a diversion to a viewpoint overlooking the deep, dramatic canyon of the Kuiseb River. During World War II two Germans, Henno Martin and Herman Korn, and their dog, used the canyon to escape internment. In 1990 their two-year adventure in the wild was finally made into a major movie, *The Sheltering Desert*.

The canyon is also home to a sub-species of desert baboon, three small but distinct troops which forage there. The so-called 'lower' troop differs from the

Following Pages: Early morning sun creates a haunting essay in light and shade among the daunting sand mountains of Sossusvlei in Namibia's Namib-Naukluft National Park.

Above: Salt pans and desert oases at the centre of the mighty rolling mountains of sand of Sossusvlei.

Opposite: Skeletal remains of a tree in the shallows of Naute Dam.

other two because, while its habitat provides plenty of food, it has little, if any, water and roams hundreds of kilometres to find it. The troop has to survive for as long as fifteen to sixteen days without drinking water, substantially longer than any other baboons could survive. It is this, coupled with the extreme heat — as high as 59°C — that may explain the troop's extreme movements. The other two troops — the 'middle' and 'upper' — have a more limited food supply but better sources of water.

A circular trail taking in the spectacular scenery and curious landmarks — Cathedral Fountain, World's View, Quartz Valley — enhanced by waterfalls and animals, birds and plants, starts and ends at park headquarters. Among the trees are mountain thorn, resin, blue-leaved corkwood, paperbark millbush, shepherd and quiver. Many of these species are protected plants. More than fifty species of animals, one-third of them rodents, have been recorded in this area of the park which was originally proclaimed a sanctuary for Hartmann's mountain zebra.

Following Pages: Lunar landscape of Namibia's formidable Naukluft National Park.

Above: Guests on a "Sky Adventure" balloon safari, celebrate safe landing in the Namib Desert with a champagne breakfast.

There are also kudu, springbok, steenbok and klipspringer, and many small predators — wild cat, caracal, genet, jackal, bat-eared fox, Cape fox and aardwolf, while the major predator is the leopard.

Some interesting birds — almost 200 species including the hammerkop, rock runners, and many rare indigenous species of robins and hornbills — as well as raptors such as black eagle, augur buzzard and lanner falcon — make their home in the Naukluft Mountains which look down on the Sesriem Canyon.

There, the Tsauchab River suddenly plunges into a deep and narrow gorge. Gradually, as the river flows west, the gorge becomes wider and shallower until the river emerges once again onto the sandy flats beyond. Legend has it that the Sesriem Canyon got its name because early visitors and settlers tied six ox thongs, *riems*, together to lower a pail into the river 30 metres or so below. The canyon is another of the Namib's spectacular features. As the rush of water echoes off the sheer cliffs, flocks of birds flutter down to drink their fill. It is thought that before

Opposite: Deep-set footprints mark a stamina-sapping ascent of one of the Namib Desert's 305-metre mountains of sand at Sossusvlei.

Above: Dwarfed by mighty dunes, camel thorns mark the course of a seasonal river in Sossusvlei.

the course of the Tsauchab River was blocked by the drifting desert dunes it emptied into the Atlantic. Now it winds sixty-five kilometres south-west through a valley of mountainous, apricot-coloured sand dunes, their wrinkled ridges shadowed by the late evening light, to enter the pan of Sossusvlei.

Only occasionally, after every five or six years, does the pan fill with water. Camel thorn trees, *Acacia erioloba*, fed by its perennial aquifers, mark the course of the seasonal Tsauchab. Desert conditions have also preserved the stumps of dead acacia which last flowered along the old course of the river 500 years ago. Where the trail ends, there is a walk of four or so kilometres over a low sand ridge to the wonder of Sossusvlei. All around, the contoured ridges of sand rise up more than 305 metres, like a brown and muddy range of alpine peaks set down among a dazzling necklace of oases.

Just before sunrise these mountainous dunes, reputed to be the highest on earth — their colours and shadows changing by the hour from beige to rust-red to

Above: Lone oryx, hardy survivor of the world's oldest desert, exists on sparse desert grasses and plants.

purple — make Sossusvlei a graceful and secret place. In recent years, winter sport enthusiasts have experimented by using the sands of the dunes, sometimes fatally, as ski and toboggan slopes.

Merciless in its immensity, the great wilderness stretches north to touch one of Namibia's great bird sanctuaries, yet another jewel in the crown of the Namib-Naukluft Park. Peerless Sandwich Harbour, a large saltwater lagoon, forty kilometres south of Walvis Bay, is home to an incredible variety of bird life. Drawn to its reed-lined pools and mud flats, pelicans, flamingo, waders and a miscellany of resident and visiting birds strut along the shores and shallows. They provide a colourful comparison to the dunes rising above them, making a superb vantage point for bird lovers. The sheltered anchorage was used by whalers in the early eighteenth century and developed into a small station also trading in seal pelts, guano and fish. The guano, an accumulation of thousands of years of bird droppings, was mined until the harbour silted up early this century. Now rusting

Above: German fortress in Africa — fascinating twenty-two roomed Duwisib Castle, the magnificent folly of German aristocrat, Baron Hans-Heinrich von Wolf.

machinery is the only reminder of this curious industry, immortalised by C. J. Andersson in *The Okavango River*:

There's an island that lies on West Africa's shore,
Where the penguins have lived since the flood or before,
And raised up a hill there, a mile high or more,
This hill is all guano, and lately 'tis shown,
That finer potatoes and turnips are grown,
By means of this compost, than ever were known;
And the peach and the nectarine, the apple, the pear,
Attain such a size that the gardeners stare,
And cry, 'Well! I never saw fruit like that 'ere!'
One cabbage thus reared, as a paper maintains,
Weighed twenty-one stone, thirteen pounds and six grains,
So no wonder guano celebrity gains.

Following Pages: A confetti shower of flamingos take-off from the Walvis Bay bird sanctuary, home to at least half the subcontinent's flamingo population.

Above: Interior detail of Duwisib Castle. Built by Baron Hans-Heinrich von Wolf in 1908-9, it is one of Namibia's most unexpected sights.

North of Sandwich Harbour, Walvis Bay, the Bay of Whales which covers 1,124 square kilometres, has been a strategic port for more than two centuries. The largest, and one of the deepest, natural harbours on Africa's south-west coast, it was formed by the delta of the Kuiseb River. Now the river seldom flows beyond Rooibank where it disappears beneath the sand to form a desert aquifer. In 1487 Bartholomeo Diaz named the bay *Golfo de Santa Maria de Conceicoa*. But when it became a whaling station the name changed. The Dutch flag flew above it for two years in the eighteenth century before the British laid claim in 1878. Half a century later it was annexed by Cape Colony, becoming part of South Africa. Until 1993 it was one of southern Africa's great anomalies, having remained under the sole jurisdiction of South Africa for three years after Namibia's independence. Nonetheless, this attractive port town has always been the gateway to South West Africa and Namibia and the main outlet to the world. Deep-sea trawlers line its stone breakwaters while, out at sea, man-made platforms collect thousands of bird

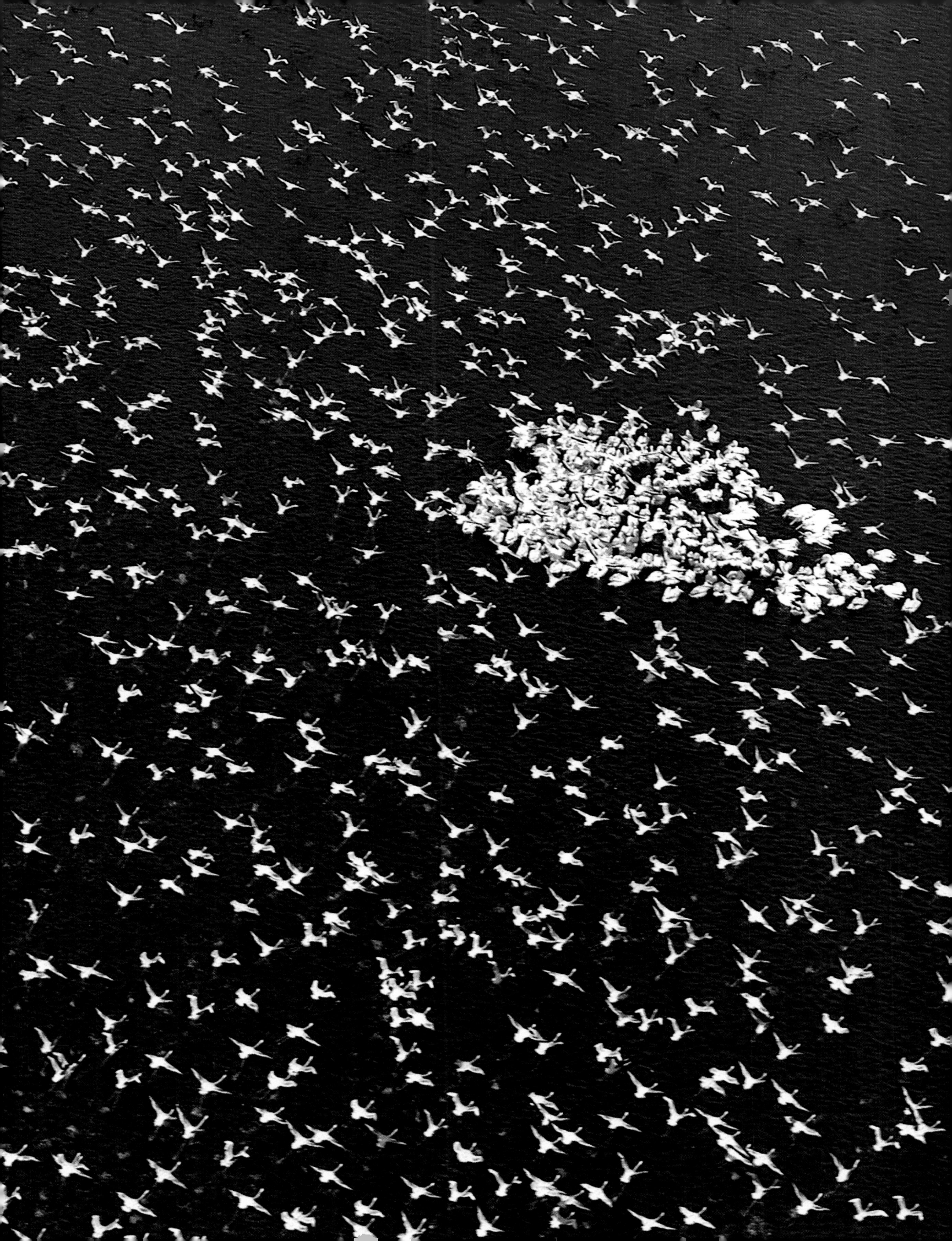

Following Pages: Majestic dunes roll down to the crystal waters of Sandwich Harbour, creating a flamingo paradise.

Above: Container vessels line the wharf at Walvis Bay, curious anachronism of South Africa's long, illegal rule over South West Africa.

Opposite: White pelican on take-off above the waters of Sandwich Harbour, one of southern Africa's greatest natural bird sanctaries.

droppings to maintain the guano industry. Boreholes in the bed of the Kuiseb river feed the town with fresh water. Gardeners suffer from the ground water in the town — four and a half times saltier than the sea — so that they can only cultivate plants with shallow root systems.

The verdant lawns outside the elegant library, however, testify to the skill of the municipal gardener. The town's oldest building, the timber Rhenish Mission Church built in Germany, dismantled and reassembled in Walvis Bay in 1880, is now a national monument.

Throughout the year the skies above the town echo to the cry of countless water birds. Indeed, Walvis Bay is an important coastal wetland and, like Sandwich Harbour, has a diverse and prolific bird population. Half the world's chestnut-banded plover live at Walvis Bay, as well great numbers of flamingo — 23,000 greater flamingo and 33,000 lesser flamingo. Like the rest of the Namib, however, the subtle Walvis Bay ecosystem can be irreparably damaged by the slightest

Above: Flamingos fill the air and cover the tidal flats of the bird sanctuary of Walvis Bay, some kilometres north of Sandwich Harbour.

change. The birds and this habitat are protected and conserved but other desert creatures have paid for mankind's greed and ruthlessness.

Elephants once roamed all over the region. In 1793 Pieter Pienaar, an early pioneer, shot three elephants and twelve rhino along the estuary of the Swakop River. Early nineteenth-century missionaries and explorers all documented vast herds of big game in the Swakop Valley. But by 1850 there was not a single elephant left in the valley or the countryside surrounding Walvis Bay. All that shows these creatures once existed are a few timeless reminders of their grace. One is a set of elephant footprints, dating back 200 or more years, embedded in clay near some dunes south of the Kuiseb River, as clear as the day the impressions were made. Another is an ancient elephant skeleton discovered near Walvis Bay in 1981.

With its attractive and majestic German colonial buildings, the charming town of Swakopmund, thirty-five kilometres north of Walvis Bay, seems much older than 100 years. But it was founded in 1892 to protect Germany's colonial interests.

Above: A mountain of salt at the Walvis Bay salt works, which covers 3,500 hectares.

The annexation of Walvis Bay by Cape Colony had left them without a port on the Atlantic. Swakopmund was planned to be that port. The first building, an army barracks, went up in July 1892, and the town's early years were a far cry from the luxurious lifestyle of today's citizens. Everything had to be brought ashore by raft, including livestock. To overcome this problem the Germans spent the enormous sum of two and a half million marks to build a breakwater. The artificial harbour basin presented the engineers with great difficulties. The stone pier, jutting more than 305 metres into the Atlantic, took years to build and was only finished in 1903. Its landward side was dominated by a slender twenty-metre lighthouse, its beam visible fifty kilometres out to sea, that still towers over the seafront. Ironically, the construction was all for naught. The seasonal Swakop river caused massive siltation and no ship could berth alongside it. Now the shallow water and beaches of the old harbour are a popular swimming spot. And the long jetty (built to replace the "mole" in 1911 but never finished) is a pier on which to walk, fish or simply

Opposite: Swakopmund's grand Kaiserliches Bezirksgericht, once a magistrate's court, is now the summer holiday home for Namibia's president.

Above: Strand Hotel at Swakopmund overlooks the town's golden beaches.

watch the sun melt into the Atlantic. Even without the flame-red sunsets that draw so many visitors, Swakopmund would be a bewitching town. And it remains a favourite South African holiday resort, complete with angling, crayfishing and many other sports.

To the north, where the Atlantic drains into huge salt pans, between 180,000 and 200,000 tonnes of salt a year are recovered — in what is virtually the town's only industry apart from domestic and international tourism. North-east of the town is Namibia's largest uranium mine. The open-cast workings at Rössing were first developed in 1973. Every week a million tonnes of ore and waste are moved, blasted, crushed and washed to produce around 3,500 tonnes of uranium oxide a year.

Swakopmund's beautifully preserved buildings reflect its imperial past at the hub of German South West Africa. Gabled tea rooms, Bavarian taverns, antique emporia crammed with memorabilia and signposts — inscribed in classic German

SWAKOPMUND PRISON

Opposite: *Swakopmund's prison, built by Heinrich Bause in 1909, is redolent of German colonialism and seems anything but a jail.*

Above: Semi-tropical plants and flowering trees keep Swakopmund in a dazzling mantle of colour all year round.

script — all bring the past to vivid life. To these have been added modern holiday homes, for Swakopmund's population doubles during summer months with thousands of holidaymakers from Windhoek and South Africa. The waterfront and suburbs are lined with neat, thatched cottages and elegant holiday homes. All have well-groomed lawns and in summer the smell of newly-cut grass hangs in the air. The town takes its name from the Swakop River which, in season, flows to the Atlantic from a great distance inland. In fact, Swakop derives from two vernacular words which describe the qualities of the raging river in spate.

As a gentle, late afternoon breeze stirs the Namibian flag, old folk take a stroll down *Bismarck Strasse* and *Kaiser Wilhelm Strasse* beneath the lengthening shadows of the palm trees — pausing to rest on benches and reminisce about the good old days. All around them are the manicured lawns and colourful flowerbeds evocative of a more gracious past. Swakopmund's finest buildings belong to the first decade of this century. Among the most outstanding examples of early German colonial architecture is the old 1901 district court building, *Bezirksgericht*. Now painted cream and green, a square tower dominates its south-east corner, and lush thick palms provide shade in its colourful gardens. It later became the official holiday residence of the German governor of South West Africa and is now the summer residence of the President. Many old buildings in Lüderitz, Walvis Bay and Swakopmund are evocative of Germany's Rhine Valley. With its medieval timber latticework, the *Woermannhaus*, the 1894 Swakopmund headquarters of the Hamburg-based Damaraland Namaqua Trading Company, is straight off a Hollywood set designer's drawing board. Lovingly preserved, it's now an arts centre and library. The square tower that abuts it served a twin-purpose as a water tower and lookout to control the movements of ships entering the harbour.

The buildings line wide and graceful avenues and malls that give a great — and sometimes incongruous — feeling of space in such a small town. Until recently, many buildings served their original purpose, the St. Antonius Hospital and the Old Post Office, for instance. But none matches the magnificent grandeur of the railway station with its green roofs, white picket fence and two vast wings, completed in 1901.

Before that, in the last century, ox-wagons took between two and three perilous weeks to travel through the Swakop Valley up to Windhoek. Lack of fodder and water, together with the scorching days and freezing nights, meant that many oxen, forced to pull heavy-laden wagons, perished. Lieutenant Edmund Troost of the imperial *Schutztruppe* found their suffering more than he could bear. On a visit to Halberstadt in 1896 he thought he had found the answer — a steam traction engine. Troost shipped it to Swakopmund where it stayed aboard ship until they could find a way to bring it ashore. When they did, the traction engine kept sinking into the mud. And once on land it was of no use at all. Its boiler needed that precious commodity — water — vast amounts of which had to be carried thirty kilometres

Opposite: Brightly-coloured flowers provide a colourful setting for elegant holiday homes at Walvis Bay.

Above: Corroded ruins of the Martin Luther *steam traction engine, now preserved as a national monument on the spot outside Swakopmund where it made its last ill-fated run in the first decade of this century.*

at thirty marks a litre. When it was finally abandoned it was named the *Martin Luther* in memory of the reformer's words: "Here I stand; God help me, I cannot do otherwise." In 1975 the corroded wreck, its wheels and boiler pockmarked with holes, became a national monument. Surrounded by palm trees, it makes an odd sight standing on its plinth in a flat, barren plain just outside town.

From the centre of Swakopmund, where you can see the sand edging ever closer to the town, the Namib stretches eastwards to the foothills of the central plateau. Herds of gemsbok and springbok roam the Namib's arid interior plains where grows one of the oldest and most remarkable plants in the world. Of all the desert's endemic plants — indeed, perhaps of all African plants — none is quite so primeval as the truly enchanting *Welwitschia mirabilis*. Some of these extraordinary plants took root more than 2,000 years ago. Myth has it that when Friedrich Welwitsch, an Austrian botanist and medical doctor, discovered the plants in 1859 in Southern Angola, he fell to his knees in stupefaction.

Above: Beacon to hundreds of ships in the dangerous storm-tossed waters of Namibia's forbidding Atlantic coastline, a 20-metre lighthouse has kept sentinel over Swakopmund throughout the twentieth century.

Since then the botanical world has quarrelled over its classification. For although a tree, the *Welwitschia* has all the traits of a flower and the primitive characteristics of a club moss. It's also a dwarf — evolution causing it to shrink in its dry, hostile environment. Existing only in a narrow belt of the Namib as far south as Swakopmund, the more you look at this living fossil, the more bizarre it becomes. There are even male and female trees. Its shallow roots search for moisture from the air, not the ground, and its saucer-shaped crown, in fact, is its trunk. Another peculiarity is that it only has two leaves which become a tangled mass that falls in all directions. They grow up to three metres long but are shredded by the wind. The female has large, blue-green seed-bearing cones that emit a sticky fluid to catch male pollen. The male's salmon-coloured cones, smaller than those of the female, release a great amount of pollen which drifts on the wind, across the plains where the trees grow, in search of a female *Welwitschia* plant.

But while *Welwitschia* collects moisture through its leaves, one of the most common dune grasses, *Stipagrostis sabulicola*, absorbs water through its shallow roots which grow just beneath the surface of the dune.

The extreme aridity of the Namib has encouraged a fine degree of specialisation. Endemic to the dunes, and found almost throughout the Namib in the vicinity of river courses, the Narra melon, *Acanthosicyos horrida*, is another plant discovered by Friedrich Welwitsch. A member of the cucumber family, its long tap root probes deep down beneath the desert in search of water — while its leafless photosynthetic stems and paired thorns cut water losses to the minimum.

The fruit of the Narra is critical to the survival of the people and wildlife which live along the Kuiseb River. Archaeological excavations of the Namib's ancient desert shelters reveal that this dependence stretches back to prehistoric times.

Indeed, so specialised are the plants of the Namib that Britain's Kew Gardens sent a special expedition into the desert to collect rare seeds to preserve for posterity in Kew's seed bank. Organised by the International Board for Genetic Resources, other seeds were taken to a regional seed bank in Lusaka, Zambia.

With more than a quarter-of-a-million plant families throughout the world, seed banks at least provide an option for survival when no other means are available. The seeds are kept in deep freeze until needed. And as insurance against environmental destruction, Kew officials were delighted with seeds of Namibia's widespread grapple plant, *Harpagophytum procumbens*, now endangered because of demand for its medicinal properties used in relieving arthritis.

The harshness of the Namib has produced a variety of remarkable plants with amazing defences against the desert. A number of odd-shaped succulents store water in their stems or leaves, or both, while euphorbias, aloes and trees develop massive trunks as reservoirs against drought.

The dwarf shrubs endemic to the northern Cape and southern Namib, with bright flowers and fleshy leaves, are critical to the survival of many desert-dwelling

Below left: Welwitschia mirabilis, *one of the world's most curious plants, found only in a limited area of southern Angola and western Namibia. Extremely long-lived, the oldest surviving specimen is thought to have first taken root 2,000 years ago.*

Below: Castles of Clay: Namib's massive termite mounds are spectacular works of natural architecture, providing air-conditioning and life-support systems for colonies of termites.

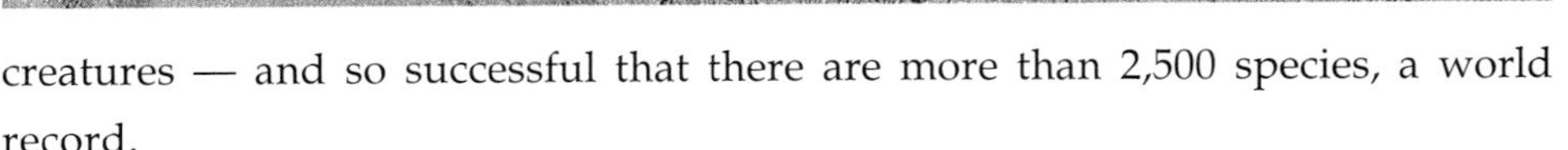

creatures — and so successful that there are more than 2,500 species, a world record.

One of their specialities is that they produce leaves only when there is enough rain, while other plants are evergreens. Acacia, with their typically small leaves, are a perfect example of adaptation to arid and semi-arid conditions.

As a result, on average, root systems of desert plants are three times larger than the mass that shows above ground. Because of this, most grow extremely slowly and produce far fewer offspring than plants with an assured source of regular water. They have one other advantage — longevity. It's hard to believe but many of the plants visitors see, particularly on the Namib's gravel plains, are already centuries old.

Other plants live out the drought in limbo as tubers and bulbs that burst into glorious life after a flush of rain. Animals which eat these dormant plants, known as *hytes*, often die of poisoning.

Above: Aloe asperifolia*, a thriving succulent endemic to the Namib Desert.*

Ephemerals are another plant group which wax and wane with rain, surviving in between by means of seeds left on top of the surface and also buried within it.

For plant lovers, the complex and sophisticated survival systems of desert species provide a unique glimpse of nature's remarkable ability to adapt to an environment as well as shape it.

Beyond the *Welwitschia* plains the road from Swakopmund climbs through the moonscape of the Swakop River Canyon, a mass of raddled rock, to the lush green oasis of Goanikontes Farm, sheltering at the foot of a great rock bluff that rises sheer for several hundred metres.

Opposite: Single-stemmed desert flower, a recognisable member of the onion family.

SWABOU
DIE MEUBELMARK

4·CASTLES IN THE SKY

Previous pages: Colourful Christmas lights bring the Namibian capital of Windhoek blazing to life during the festive season.

Opposite: Tiny narrow-gauge 1903 locomotive outside Windhoek's impressive mainline station.

Early morning, with its crisp air, brings promise of another sparkling day in Namibia's capital. Barely more than a century old, Windhoek is driven by youthful vigour — fuelled by its coming of age in 1990.

Sheltered as it is between the Eros and Auas mountains, 1,646 metres above sea level, wherever you look there are magnificent, unspoilt panoramas and in every direction the lure of distant horizons.

Few of the world's capitals demonstrate their civic pride so conspicuously. This cosmopolitan metropolis is free from litter, pollution, traffic jams and graffiti. It is so immaculate that "swept-clean" hardly does justice to its sparkling streets and sidewalks lined with dazzling flowerbeds. But something else sets it apart from any other African capital — a touch of medieval fantasy. Three castles, Schwerinsburg, Heinitzburg and Sanderburg, stand on the hills overlooking downtown Windhoek. While clocktowers that keep perfect time watch over shops crammed with the latest Paris fashions, gemstones the size of grapes, and banks with cash dispensers, along the warm, sunny streets, hawkers and bohemians mix with city and country folk against a canvas of contemporary and colonial architecture. Alfresco cafés on the pavements and balconies serve beer brewed according to the medieval Purity Law of ancient Germany, and the world's finest wines.

Art galleries exhibit the works of international artists alongside those of Namibian painters and sculptors. On the sidewalks and at craft centres, vendors display local soapstone sculptures, carved wooden masks and Herero dolls in Victorian dress. But despite its skyscrapers Windhoek is uniquely African — and growing at an astonishing rate.

The catalyst for this rapid development was the moment when independence dawned in 1990. Now Windhoek's ever-increasing prosperity together with an infrastructure that is the envy of many in the Western world, reflects the hopes and aspirations which are driving Namibia into the twenty-first century. Yet for all that, the capital retains the ambience of its colonial German heritage.

The early history of Windhoek revolved around a number of hot, warm and cold springs, which were previously found in the area. It was the occurrence of these springs that led the Nama to give the area the name *Ai-gams*, meaning "water of fire"; while the Hereros knew it as *Otjomuise*, meaning "place of steam". The Oorlam leader Jan Jonker Afrikaner, who settled in 1840, called it Winterhoek, which means "winter corner" — after his birthplace, near Winterhoekberg. But after Jonker's death in 1861, Windhoek was left virtually abandoned. In 1873 missionary Hugo Hahn noted that Windhoek's beautiful wooded valley, encircled by hills, had changed for the worse. The magnificent trees near the warm springs on the mountains to the south had been uprooted by strong winds and the Nama. Soon after, the Herero, under Maherero, took possession and, when the Nama responded, Windhoek was devastated and left

Opposite: Now preserved on an island in downtown Windhoek's modern thoroughfare, the capital's elegant 1907 Christuskirche was designed by architect Gottlieb Redecker with typical Teutonic grandeur.

deserted. But in October 1890, German officials laid the foundation stone for a fortress there and established a garrison of stormtroopers. It marked the birth of this new capital and once again the neglected gardens of abandoned missions bloomed. Drawn by the promise of farmland, settlers began to flood in from Germany and South Africa and Windhoek grew swiftly.

Above: Kalahari Sands Hotel, regarded as the finest in the capital, stands at the heart of Independence Avenue — Windhoek's main street.

The three castles were among its earliest buildings. The first was built as a watchtower in 1891 by Captain Curt von Francois. It was then bought by Graf von Schwerin who turned it into a fort and named it Schwerinsburg after his grandfather. He later commissioned a second castle by an architect called Sander, who followed this up by building his own version.

By the turn of the century, the capital had a dozen permanent shops which quickly multiplied with the arrival of the railway in 1902. Above all, as everywhere else in this fascinating new country, there was space. Wide and handsome streets gave new perspectives for buildings in the German colonial

Following Pages: Windhoek is a mixture of old and new architecture. Red-roofed buildings of colonial design, skyscrapers, and, centre, the inimitable Christuskirche*: one of the finest churches in southern Africa.*

Above: Alfresco Windhoek exhibition of fragments recovered from the Gibeon meteorite shower which were scattered across 20,000 square kilometres of southern Namibia.

style, with red roofs, some pitched steep like those on the villages in the German mountains. The view is best appreciated among the rocks and thorns of the slopes above the main centre. The slender spire of the Evangelical Lutheran church is charming contrast to the high-rise hotels and offices of the last two decades. The cornerstone of *Christuskirche*, designed by Gottlieb Redecker, was laid in October 1907, and the church was consecrated in 1910. With its rounded gables, scarlet-iron roofs and soaring 43-metre spire, it is obvious that Redecker drew heavily on neo-Gothic styles for inspiration. The church was built from local limestone and the doorway was crafted from marble brought in from the famous Tuscan town of Carrara. The organ and stained glass windows came from Germany with Kaiser Wilhelm II donating the chancel windows, and his wife the altar bible.

The nearby Rider Memorial, depicting an unknown member of the German cavalry, was raised in honour of Germans killed during the Herero and Nama

Above: Herero dolls with their vivid colours on sale in Windhoek, a reminder of Victorian influence on tradition.

rebellion — in the first decade — and paid for by public subscription. It was unveiled on 27 January 1912 — Kaiser Wilhelm II's birthday.

Perhaps the building most evocative of Windhoek's early years is the 1913 multi-roofed *Gathemann Haus* on Independence Avenue (formerly *Kaiser Strasse*). Another interesting colonial structure stands at the intersection with Lüderitz Street — the old magistrate's court built in 1898. And not far away, in Leutwein Street, recently renamed Robert Mugabe Avenue, is the 1959 State House which replaced the old 1892 governor's residence. The building next to it, Dernburg House, was built in 1908 for one of the governor's aides. Another landmark in Robert Mugabe Avenue is the Ink Palace, *Tintenpalast*, so named because it housed the colonial bureaucracy. It was also designed by Redecker. When Governor von Schuckmann announced that the administrative building would stand on a knoll outside the city centre he met enormous resistance from the settlers. Completed in 1914, with its well-tended lawns and flourishing gardens,

Right: *Windhoek is adorned with numerous striking wall-paintings in an array of vibrant colours.*

the *Tintenpalast* is today officially known as the Parliament Building. The modern building next door, which houses the Office of the President, has a large mural depicting the geography and colonial history of Namibia. And just beyond that is the capital's old fort, put up in 1890 to house the first garrison.

Elizabeth House, a maternity home for more than seventy years, was another building designed by Redecker. The architect was actually born in Namibia in 1871. From the inauguration of Elizabeth House in 1908 until its closure in 1981, more than 12,000 people were born there. In fact, Windhoek grew so fast that in 1915 an annex was added to keep pace with the mushrooming population. This monument to motherhood was named after Countess Elizabeth zu Mecklenburg, wife of Count Johan Albrecht zu Mecklenburg. Since 1981 Elizabeth House has been used as a theatre, with poetry readings, musical concerts and drama.

The anticipation of independence heralded increased development and the

1980s saw the capital's skyline take shape. Skyscrapers thrust into the sky, bearing down on a concentration of new parks and piazzas. One skyscraper is the elegant Kalahari Sands Hotel where Britain's Queen Elizabeth II and Prince Philip stayed in 1991.

Despite its architecture, Windhoek remains essentially African. At almost every corner stand crafted, wide-rimmed Herero wicker baskets, proffered for sale by Herero women. They wear the Victorian costumes introduced in the name of decorum by nineteenth-century missionaries.

The city structure of Windhoek is today still influenced by the apartheid system, with its division of the black, coloured, and white populations. About half of Windhoek's population today is still living in the largely squalid area of Katutura, a name which means "place where we do not want to live". This township is in sharp contrast to the rest of the city. Its large number of squatters and shanties stand as grim testimony to the struggle for survival around which the lives of its inhabitants revolve.

One-third of Windhoek's 190,000 citizens are European. The shops and restaurants reflect this influence, while the names of the city centre's malls and avenues echo its German colonial birth. But as the mountains around Windhoek turn purple and mauve with evening, the capital's nightlife begins. Baroque classics, cabarets and dramas draw people into the theatres and restaurants — while in the discos the young of all races dance the night away. German drinking songs echo through the beer gardens and nostalgic taverns. *Gemütlichkeit*, the spirit of friendship and laughter, is everywhere.

Above: Sculpted monument topped by a carved elephant skull marks a prehistoric site in Windhoek where Stone Age tools and elephant bones were discovered.

South of Windhoek, around the thermal springs that gave the capital its existence, the sleepy spa town of Rehoboth nestles in the folds of the Auas Mountains. It has been the capital of the 40,000 Baster people for more than a century. The half-caste Basters, fathered by Dutch Boers out of African womenfolk, were shunned by Europeans and Africans. They moved north from the Cape in search of farmlands. In 1871 they established their own nation state and legislative system at Rehoboth and soon developed a strong community identity.

North of the capital, Hereroland straddles a large sandveld to the south and west of the San homelands. Before they were coerced to live in this wilderness the Herero were nomadic pastoralists grazing their cattle on southern Africa's sweeping savannahs. For decades early last century they were at war with their Nama neighbours. The bitter dispute claimed thousands of victims but the Herero more than held their own. Everything changed, however, with the advent of European colonialisation. Christian missionaries were the first to leave their mark in the shape of Victorian fashion — so outraged were they to be confronted by the unclad bodies of the Herero. Soon the ladies of the tribe were parading in the bustles and gowns of high society — and still do. In summer on

Above: Constructed in October 1890, the Alte Feste was erected as the headquarters of the Schutztruppe. It is the capital's longest surviving building.

Windhoek's crowded streets, these nineteenth-century dresses, with their voluminous petticoats, and broad, brightly-coloured headdresses, make an incongruous sight, even more so in the empty wastes of Hereroland.

The clothes did nothing to protect the community from the German colonisers who almost exterminated the tribe after it rose up in rebellion under Chief Samuel Maherero. He called on all Africans to join together to fight German enslavement. In 1904, the two sides clashed in the north in a bloody and disastrous rout for the Herero. During the next four years more than three-quarters of the men, women and children were slaughtered. The Herero were totally overwhelmed. Those who escaped were rounded up into concentration camps. The remainder fled into exile in Bechuanaland, now Botswana. And at the end of all this, General von Trotha, the German Commander, issued a proclamation which stated: 'I, the great general of the German troops, send this letter to the Herero people. Hereros are no longer German subjects . . . All the

Above: Leopard, most stealthy of Namibia's big cats, stalks through a rocky wilderness.

Hereros must leave the land . . . I will force them to do it with the great guns. Any Herero found within the German borders . . . will be shot, I shall no longer receive any women or children. I will drive them back . . . or . . . shoot them.'

Now these once-proud people and their cousins, the Mbanderu, representing about eight per cent of Namibia's population, have fallen on hard times, with many becoming destitute.

The main highway that curves along Namibia's backbone, from South Africa to Angola, touches many of the outstanding features that give the country its character and charm. Among the rolling hills of Khomas Hochland that seem to stretch westward forever, Daan Viljoen Game Reserve lies fourteen kilometres north-west of Windhoek. Named after a former administrator, D. T. du P. Viljoen, the reserve stands on the banks of the Augeigas Dam and is a peerless setting in which to study the resident wildlife. Blue wildebeest, red hartebeest, eland, kudu, gemsbok, klipspringer and zebra graze on the flaxen savannah,

Above: Leopard lured to bait for photographic enthusiasts.

while the clear waters of the dam teem with fish including black bass, kurper and barbel. More than 200 species of bird inhabit the park. A nine-kilometre nature trail takes walkers through the arid, hilly scrub to a magnificent viewpoint overlooking the capital in the distance below.

From Windhoek the main highway heads sixty-five kilometres north, along the western borders of the vast badlands of Hereroland, to Okahandja. It was there, in 1843, that two Germans, Carl Hugo Hahn and Heinrich Kleinschmidt, established a Rhenish mission station.

There were, however, few converts — for the Herero were too engrossed with their war against the Nama. But one Nama was taken by their message. Jager Afrikaner, the Nama leader, renounced the conflict to become a devoted Christian. Until then Jager, whose men were armed to the teeth, was much feared by the colonialists, but his attempts to convert his fellow Nama failed.

Jager's successor, Jonker Afrikaner, was welcomed by the Wesleyan traders

Opposite: Early Henschel heavy-duty locomotive at Otjiwarongo in northern Namibia. It was taken out of service when the narrow-gauge line was standardised in 1960.

who gave him arms, ammunition, brandy, and luxuries on credit. They encouraged him to run up a large bill which was calculated against numbers of cattle. The chief was soon in debt, but the Nama were not pastoralists and only kept small herds. In 1850, when the traders demanded payment, Jonker attacked the Herero on a low hill near the town — slaughtering the warriors, led by Chief Kahitjenne, and stealing their cattle to pay his debts.

Above: German watch tower built in 1904 to resist the aggressive intentions of the Herero.

Francis Galton, the English explorer, who had arrived in south-western Africa shortly before, posed as a government dignitary to persuade the Nama chief to order a ceasefire. Only after Galton had gone did Jonker discover that he had been conned. Furious, he went to war again. But not for long. Soon after, in October 1861, Jonker Afrikaner — perhaps Namibia's most colourful native son — died at Okahandja where his grave is now a national monument. But the town is also central to Herero culture. Indeed, each year thousands of tribespeople make a pilgrimage there to pay tribute to their dead heroes buried close to their Nama adversary.

Just a few kilometres east of the town, an eighty-nine square kilometre game ranch at Otjisazu offers hunting safaris for those who want the thrill of stalking and killing their trophies. In the 1990s, however, most people prefer to do their shooting with a camera.

Twenty-four kilometres west of Okahandja, the ruins of a Rhenish mission station, built in 1844 by Carl Hugo Hahn and Heinrich Kleinschmidt, are visible alongside the hot springs at Gross-Barmen. The mission was abandoned in 1890. The thermal springs, famed for their curative properties, are believed to ease rheumatism. As they bubble out of the ground at 65°C, they fill two swimming pools — one indoor, the other outdoor — and private baths.

There is also another road west at Okahandja which leads to Karibib to form the base of a triangle that encloses the 2,355-metre Omburo Mountains and has its apex at Otjiwarongo. From Karibib, the road that forms the western line of the triangle passes north-east through the small community of Omaruru. Extraordinary for its diversity of natural and neolithic wonders, the site has been inhabited by the San for thousands of years. Omaruru, meaning "bitter curd", derives its name because Herero cattle graze on an indigenous bush that gives their milk a sour flavour.

Europeans favoured the banks of the nearby Omaruru River, hunting mercilessly in the surrounding plains. Within a few years of their arrival, by 1880, all the elephant, rhinoceros, giraffe and lion populations had been annihilated. Settlers and their herds of livestock took the place of the great beasts which had been slaughtered. And with the 1884 declaration that South West Africa was to become a German colony, a small garrison was established at Omaruru. A decade later, when the Tsumeb-Swakopmund railway reached the town, the Herero rose up in rebellion. Three years after they were put down,

OTJIWARONGO
S.W.A.
13.11.1960

Opposite: The Catholic Church at Otjiwarongo is eclipsed only by the might of the African skies behind.

Above: The 35-metre limestone column of the Vingerklip towers over the flood plain north of the Ugab River in Namibia's northern hinterland.

in 1908, a memorial commemorating the German victory was erected. Known as the Franke Tower, after Captain Victor Franke, the edifice still stands.

Northward is the small town of Kalkeld where a dirt road leads east to Otjihaenamaparero, a farm much visited by naturalists and palaeontologists, for it gives a colourful indication of the great age of the Namibian plains. Preserved in the farm's prehistoric clays is the twenty-five-metre trail left there by a three-toed, two-legged dinosaur. Each imprint, pressed deep into the rose-coloured Etjo sandstone, was made between 185 and 150 million years ago. Gazing at these footprints, now a national monument, creates a sudden awareness of man's fragile mortality and Namibia's rich primordial legacy.

Also on the plains close by, under the brow of 2,377-metre Mount Etjo, world-renowned conservationist Jan Oelofse runs his own private Eden, a sprawling game reserve where much of Namibia's wildlife may be seen. Guests stay in the reserve's luxurious lodge overlooking a series of water-holes where

Opposite: Gravel road stretches away from the Vingerklip in the lengthening shadows of a Namibian afternoon.

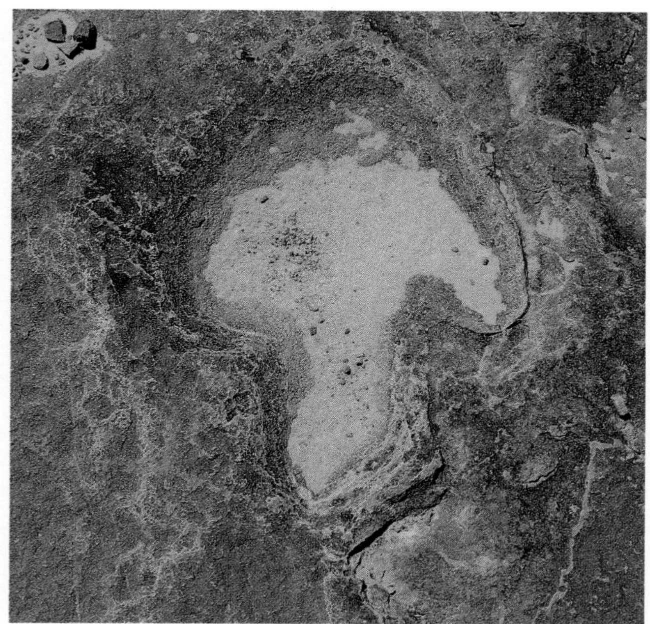

Above: Single footprint of a dinosaur, one of the Waterberg Plateau Park's very first visitors.

Right: Laurel fig tree, Ficus ilicina, *clings to one of the Waterberg Plateau Park's exquisite rock formations, set against the fabulous blue African sky.*

the animals, including elephant, come to drink. There are also treetop hides where, by the light of a full moon, the visitors observe creatures of the night. Treks into the surrounding mountains take visitors to caves with rock paintings and sites with prehistoric fossils and animal tracks.

Dinosaurs once roamed the woodlands and tawny savannahs of the Waterberg Plateau, east of Otjiwarongo. This is the town where an old mission station was established in 1891 when the missionaries signed a treaty with the Herero chief, Kambazembi. The town that grew up around the mission flourished early this century after it was linked by rail to Swakopmund and Tsumeb in April 1906. An old 1912 narrow-gauge Henschel locomotive, in use until 1960 when the track became standard gauge, stands outside the railway station.

Well to the west — midway between Outjo and Khorixas — alone and standing erect like some giant tombstone, the Rock Finger, *Vingerklip,* rises more than 34 metres into the sky, towering over the surrounding countryside. The natural obelisk is composed of red limestone.

Rising some kilometres to the east of Otjiwarongo, the Waterberg Plateau steps sheer up a 200-metre red sandstone cliff. The plateau's breathtaking and extraordinary rock formations are typical of much of central Namibia. Indeed, the region is a place of pilgrimage for geologists while much of the plateau is

Above: Classic 1953 Chevvy truck at the Immenhof Guest Farm remains in pristine condition because of Namibia's dry, non-corrosive climate.

now a park to protect some of southern Africa's most rare and endangered species. No roads scar the plateau's pristine 400 square kilometres of parched landscape with its sandstone backdrops. What few visitors there are must follow their guides across the wilderness on foot. They are resigned to trek only along natural game trails and dry water courses beneath pillars of rock to avoid lasting damage to the fragile ecology. There, white rhino and buffalo mingle with many species of antelope including roan, sable, tsessebe, blue wildebeest, steenbok, klipspringer, duiker and eland. Leopard and cheetah hunt such creatures as prey.

More than 200 species of bird have been recorded including the rare, endangered Cape vulture, Africa's second-largest vulture, which circles on the afternoon thermals. Predominantly white in appearance, adult birds have a thick naked neck, yellow eyes and three-metre wingspan. They prefer to hunt and scavenge over open, grassy hills, nesting in colonies on the inaccessible ledges of high cliffs. But they are regarded as pests by farmers who laid poison in the early 1980s to kill them off. By 1983 a mere nine birds survived. Now rangers foster their regeneration by culling antelopes and leaving the carcasses out on the plains. Happily, their numbers are increasing.

Power pylons were another threat to the survival of the Cape vulture. After several were electrocuted, South Africa's power utility modified the pylons. This not only helped vultures and other birds, but also reduced the number of power failures. Another five vultures endemic to southern Africa are endangered and among the other hunters of the sky the Bateleur eagle is also threatened.

Above: A familiar landmark fifty kilometres outside Windhoek is the red-roofed Düsternbrook guest farm, situated above a dry river bed.

Of the other vultures, the most impressive is the white-headed vulture — almost always first on a carcass because it is non-competitive — snatching what it can before the others arrive. But it also makes its own kills as does the lappet-faced vulture of the Namib.

Some 120 kilometres north-east of the plateau, along the highway, overlooked by the mountains that gave it its name, Otavi is today remembered for its Khorab Memorial. It was there, in July 1915, that the German troops surrendered to the South African forces, ending their part in World War I.

In 1908, a narrow-gauge railway linked the ninety-one kilometres from Otavi to Grootfontein in the north-east. The town takes its name from the springs in its northern suburbs. The Herero know it as the Mount of the Leopard, *Otjivandatjongue*. The sweet waters refreshed ivory hunters who decimated the region's elephant herds in the middle of the last century, and lured white settlers, including the Dorsland Trekkers, in the decades that followed. On the nearby plains, halfway between Grootfontein and Tsumeb, stands one of the wonders of the world — a cuboid, fifty-tonne meteorite, the largest on earth which collided with our planet about 30,000 years ago. It was discovered at Hoba Farm in 1920 by Jacobus Brits while he was hunting. He was so intrigued by this unusual half-buried rock that he chiselled off a piece and took it to experts at Grootfontein. Analysis showed it was truly out of this world. It contained eighty-two per cent iron, sixteen per cent nickel and small amounts of many other metals — such as cobalt, iridium, germanium and gallium. The general manager of the South West Africa Company wanted to extract the meteorite's nickel but common sense prevailed. Nonetheless, even though it was

Above: Lush leaves cast a mantle of shade over the banks of Otjikoto Lake, near the mining town of Tsumeb in northern Namibia. It was formed after the roof of an underground cavern collapsed.

declared a national monument in 1955, it has been badly despoiled by souvenir hunters. Since 1985, however, it has been kept under vigil to prevent any more vandalism.

The northern extremity of Hereroland is marked by the mining town of Tsumeb with its white one-storey buildings. One of the most important mineralogical centres in the world, Tsumeb lies between Etosha National Park to the west, Kavango to the north and Bushmanland to the east. The land around the town is rich with mineral wealth. More than 180 minerals, including ten metal ores found nowhere else on earth, have been identified, but only eighteen are exploited. Moreover, the mine is the source of all kinds of beautiful rocks, crystals and gemstones. Many rare minerals — Smithsonite on Willemite, mottrammite and calite, rich in pastel yellows, olive greens and abstract formations — are on display in Tsumeb museum. But the most complete collection is housed in the Museum of Natural History in the Smithsonian

Above: Relics of pioneering days and old farm equipment decorate a rest camp at Khorixas.

Institute in Washington, USA. The Tsumeb museum also has a display of German cannons recovered from the fifty-five-metre depths of Lake Otjikoto where troops dumped them and their ammunition before surrendering in World War I. The lake's clear waters supply the town, irrigate surrounding farmlands and contain several fish species including two rare mouth-breeders. The sunken lake formed when the roof of a huge dolomite cave collapsed.

Tsumeb's industrial legacy has done no damage to the town's charm. The dazzling arrays of flamboyants, bougainvillea and jacarandas lining the streets cast a profusion of colour over the town.

The north-western extremity of the Kalahari thrusts eastward from Tsumeb, beginning at the banks of the Omatako River. Fable says that lost somewhere among the sands of the Kalahari are the ruins of a great city. One who claimed to have found them was a nineteenth-century conman, William Leonard Hunt, who later wrote *Through the Kalahari Desert*.

Above: Victorian steam traction engine preserved outside the museum in the mining centre of Tsumeb, northern Namibia.

'We camped . . . beside a long line of stone which looked like the Chinese Wall after an earthquake, and which, on examination, proved to be the ruins of quite an extensive structure, in some places buried beneath the sand, but in others fully exposed to view. We traced the remains for nearly a mile, mostly a heap of huge stones, but all flat-sided, and here and there with the cement perfect and plainly visible between the layers. . . . The general outline of this wall was in the form of an arc, inside which lay at intervals of about forty feet apart a series of heaps of masonry in the shape of an oval or obtuse ellipse, about a foot and a half deep, and with a flat bottom, but hollowed out at the sides for about a foot from the edge. Some of these heaps were cut out of solid rock, others were formed of more than one piece of stone, fitted together very accurately. . . . On digging down nearby in the middle of the arc, we came upon a pavement about twenty feet wide, made of large stones. . . . This pavement was intersected by another similar one at right angles,

Above: Slender lines of soaring spire grace exterior of a modern church at Outjo town in northern Namibia.

forming a Maltese cross, in the centre of which at some time must have stood an altar, column, or some sort of monument, for the base was quite distinct, composed of loose pieces of fluted masonry.'

Although it was impossible to have made the journey in the short time given, the account and illustrations inspired many to search for this desert Atlantis. As did the poetry.

A half-buried ruin — a huge wreck of stones
On a lone and desolate spot;
A temple — or a tomb for human bones
Left by man to decay and rot.
Rude sculptured blocks from the red sand project,
And shapeless uncouth stones appear,
Some great man's ashes designed to protect,
Buried many a thousand year.
A relic, may be, of the glorious past,
A city once grand and sublime,
Destroyed by earthquake, defaced by the blast,
Swept away by the hand of time.

Taunted throughout summer by the dark clouds that soar across the sky, always promising, rarely delivering, the Kalahari receives little more than 150 millimetres of rain a year. For thousands of years the desert, which stretches from Namibia all across Botswana to Zimbabwe, and from the Okavango Delta to the Orange River, has been the ancestral home of the renowned trackers and hunters of the San. Immortalised by many writers, including the South African poet Laurens van der Post, they are also known as the Bushmen.

Dramatic change in the culture of these nomadic hunter-gatherers came in the 1980s when the Bushman Development Foundation was established to focus on pastoralism and small-scale farming. Now Namibia's Bushmen endeavour to cling to their ancient ways in small settlements scattered across the flaxen, acacia veld of the Kalahari.

Their fragile culture has been under siege since they first came in contact with other people. This happened after the influx of Nama pastoralists, themselves descendants of the Khoikhoi of the Cape Province, during the early eighteenth century. The troubles of these peaceful people were then compounded when the Wambo and Bergdama tribes swept in behind the Nama; as the Bantu-speaking Herero filtered into the Kunene Region in north-west Namibia, before moving down the centre of the country. Finally, large numbers of the Oorlam tribe advanced into Namibia's heartlands, bringing with them Western weapons. In *The Harmless People,* Elizabeth Marshall notes: 'Bushmen would not

Above: Sylvan delights of Tsumeb's verdant municipal park in one of the world's most pleasant industrial towns.

try to fight because they have no mechanism . . . for dealing with disagreements other than to remove the cause of the disagreements. Their hold on life is too tenuous to permit quarrelling among themselves. A Bushman will go to any lengths to avoid making other Bushmen jealous. . . . Their culture insists that they share with one another. . . .'

The San once populated the whole of southern Africa but were driven back deep into the desert by the encroaching colonials. In *South West Africa,* Ruth First said of this singular race: 'Today in South West Africa small remnants . . . roam the banks of the Orange River, the Namib desert, and the wastes of the north-east adjoining Ovamboland [now Kunene]. But the greatest numbers struggle to survive in the Kalahari desert, the no-man's-land between South West Africa and Bechuanaland that no one else wants.'

As recently as the 1950s, light-coloured, fine-boned San stalked game in the tall grasses of Bushmanland, in what are now the Otjozondjupa and Omaheke

Regions — on the Kalahari's western edges — with their poisoned arrows. But with the white settlers encroaching into their land the Bushmen moved deeper and deeper into the inhospitable drylands.

The San's mystic communion with the wilderness and its creatures has long fascinated observers. But ignorance and misunderstanding of their life, particularly by the missionaries, was profound. San bushcraft is unique. These small, hardy people are able to identify the spoor of any creature and track them enormous distances through the uncharted wastes of the Kalahari, defying scorching sun and freezing nights in a remarkable display of endurance. In a land of extremely limited resources, the San exploit every option. They also have an uncanny ability for detecting underground water and know every plant in their world and the uses to which they can be put. Poison for their arrows, made from snake venom, extracted from scorpions or tapped from the sap of desert trees, kills even elephant in seconds. Their seemingly random desert trails take advantage of scarce water and seasonal fruits.

San folklore, handed down orally from generation to generation, is rich with religious allegory and allusion. Hypnosis by holy men, *shamans*, is performed to cure illnesses and relieve suffering, the medium often entering a catatonic state as onlookers sing, dance and clap.

Experts believe the San artists who executed rock paintings and carvings all over southern Africa were often in such a delirium. The San were trading with Bantu tribes 2,000 years ago and adopted many customs and traditions, including keeping livestock. Thanks to intermarriage with other southern groups, the distinctive San "click" language was adopted by groups such as the Zulu and Xhosa. And modern research now indicates that European pioneers were wrong to regard the San as an isolated neolithic race. The pace of colonisation altered San life irrevocably as their communities were pushed ever backward until they disappeared or sought refuge in the inner Kalahari wilderness. The San who have survived and transformed, moving away from the traditions that ensured their society's survival for thousands of years, are now forging a new destiny in a modern world. But all should lament what has been lost.

5 · SKELETON

COAST, PETRIFIED FOREST

Previous pages: Quintessential Namibian landscape where sand and scrubland meld in pastel perfection.

Where the icy Atlantic waves tear at Namibia's jagged coastline, a great cross, chiselled from black rock, looks out to the storm-tossed horizon. The crucifix is a replica of the one placed there more than 500 years ago by navigator-explorer Diego Cão. He was ordered by the King of Portugal to round the southern cape of Africa and discover a sea route to the spice centres of the East. Thus, six years before Columbus stepped ashore in the New World, Cão sailed from Lisbon.

A knight of the Portuguese Court and a great seaman, Cão was given two stone crosses, *padrãos,* hewn from Lisbon's finest rock, to raise up on new-found shores — in the name of Portugal, King John II and Christianity. He was told not to return until his mission was accomplished. It is easy to imagine the horrific conditions at sea in the fifteenth century when crews perished from a combination of scurvy, plague and lack of fresh water. Although Cão's small fleet braved the stormy waters of the South Atlantic for well on two years, his expedition ended in failure. Fearful of the monarch's wrath, the explorer contrived to pitch one cross at the mouth of the Congo River, while the other was raised on the coastline at *Cabo do Lobo,* now *Cabo do Santa Maria* in Angola. There, out of food and drinking water, the barren shores seeming to stretch forever southwards, Cão turned round and headed home to face the anger of the King. Failure however was not in the royal lexicon. Cão was handed another pair of crosses, given two new ships and sent on his way again.

Above: Cape Cross monument to Diego Cão, first European to set foot on Namibian shores.

The navigator embarked on this second voyage with heavy heart as he once more charted his way southwards through the storm-tossed Atlantic. Eventually he arrived at the barren stretch of forbidding land bordered by endless hostile shores. History records that by this time Cão was a broken man. Choosing a rocky cape that jutted out into the dark seascape, he anchored there briefly in January 1486, to step ashore and set up one of the crosses; before returning despondent and humiliated to his death aboard his ship on the voyage home to Portugal. The Portuguese inscription on the cross read:

'In the year 6685 of the creation of the earth and 1485 after the birth of Christ the most excellent and most serene King Dom Jovo II of Portugal ordered this land to be discovered and this *padrão* to be placed by Diego Cão, gentleman of his house.'

The cross stood atop the barren cape to which it gave its name, all the world unheeding of its existence, for almost 400 years, until the middle of the last century. It was then seen by Captain W. Messum who was combing the seaboard for guano deposits. These led to an influx of European sailing ships along Namibia's coast hauling away tons of the fertiliser in a 'guano rush' akin to the gold rush of Johannesburg.

Thirty years later, in 1879, W. B. Warren, captain of the cruiser *Swallow,* was searching for a place to land when he saw Cão's cross. The skipper had a German concession to work the guano deposits and hunt seals along the coast

Opposite: Rock solid, a giant Cape fur seal basks on the shore at Cape Cross.

between the Ugab and Omaruru Rivers. In 1895, sixteen years after he first landed, he laid a small railway near Cape Cross which presented its builders with an extraordinary challenge. It fell into disrepair in 1906 but its remains on the salt-pans of Cape Cross are still visible.

After facing centuries of cruel winds, Cão's stone cross developed a severe list and was in danger of collapse. But early in 1893 the captain of the German cruiser *Falke* recognised its historical importance and took it away leaving a wooden replica in its place. Two years later that was replaced by a granite replica bearing the original Portuguese inscription, plus another in German, under the Kaiser's eagle. It read: 'Erected by order of the German Kaiser and King of Prussia Wilhelm II in 1894 at the place of the original which has been weathered through years.' The *Falke* carried the cruciform to Cape Town, the destination that Diego Cão had striven to reach but failed. From there it was taken to a Berlin museum.

Above: Visitors to the Skeleton Coast enjoy a drive along the edge of the icy Atlantic waves.

Above: Cape fur seals at Cape Frio on the Skeleton Coast seem to thrive on one of Africa's most inhospitable stretches of seaboard.

The rocks below Cape Cross are alive with a multitude of Cape fur seal cows whose cries and barks fill the air. Around 90,000 creatures, there to give birth, jostle for a precious but precarious flipper hold on the rocky shore. When the males travel far off into the South Atlantic at the end of each breeding season, they are already twice as heavy, at 190 kilos, as the cows. By eating the equivalent of eight per cent of their body weight each day the bulls take full advantage of the Atlantic's rich marine life to virtually double their weight to 360 kilos. Then, as the October winds south of the Equator carry the first nascent promise of southern spring, the great bulls begin to arrive at the end of their 1,600-kilometre odyssey from the south. They are ready to establish a brood of between five and twenty-five cows and to protect their domains. Although sleek and elegant in the water, on land the great bulls are cumbersome and awkward. In the next six weeks they burn the extra fat away in vicious fights with their rivals — snarling and rearing up aggressively,

Above: Parched and cracked desert terrain where only flora and fauna which are specially adapted to these unforgiving conditions can survive.

lunging their heads and snapping their teeth in an awesome display of might. At the end the vanquished lurch away in shame.

Most Cape fur seal pups are born in late November and early December, after a nine-month gestation. The tiny, black, new-born blubbery forms wriggle helplessly in all directions. The icy waters teem with female seals catching fish for their offspring. Left alone, the pups are tempting prey for the Namib's hungry hunter-scavengers — black-backed jackal and brown hyena. And the unwieldy and careless movements of the great bulls leave hundreds more squashed in their wake. Every December dozens of dead calves litter the shore in feast for the scavengers. When the cows return from fishing they trace their siblings through a combination of wailing and scent. Within days of giving birth the cows mate again with the bulls. For many observers, however, what lingers most is the appalling stench that emanates from this mass of blubber. Nonetheless, it does nothing to deter the hunters who cull the seals each year.

Above: Natural rock arch on the Spitzkoppe massif.

Layers of hair, fur and blubber form an effective insulation system to protect the sleek creatures from the freezing waters of the Benguela Current. An outer mantle of coarse, protective hair acts as waterproofing, beneath which a thick blanket of fur remains dry. Air trapped inside the fur serves as a form of double-glazing that keeps out the cold. Their blood is so warm, however, that instead of freezing in the water the seals suffer from the heat of the shore. As a result they have developed sweat glands on bare areas and in their flippers. And the massive bull seals often dig their enormous flippers deep into the sand to keep them cool.

Cape Cross stands in the centre of the National West Coast Recreational Area which stretches 200 kilometres. It forms a broad band more than fifty kilometres across from Swakopmund in the south to the Ugab River — and the borders of the Skeleton Coast Park in the north. The coast is an angler's paradise with camping facilities spread along the shoreline. Swakopmund is the main centre

Opposite: *Granite boulders mark the base of Spitzkoppe — the Matterhorn of southern Africa.*

Above: German watch tower, built by soldiers in 1902 at Outjo town.

but Henties Bay, discovered in 1929, is also a favourite. Its population of 1,500 increases tenfold in the high summer months.

But outside the resorts — with their modern amenities — simple survival is the greatest challenge facing the small communities which live across much of this harsh north-western wilderness. The coast's sparsely populated hinterland forms the vast Kaokoveld, renamed Kunene in 1993. It reaches hundreds of kilometres inland as far as Outjo and north-east beyond Etosha, including 50,000 square kilometres of what was Kaokoland in the north.

In the south, Damaraland, renamed Erongo, is sandwiched between the Namib Desert in the west and the 2,438-metre Paresis Mountains in the east. While the Damara speak the Nama language, their physical appearance is more like that of the people of central Africa. It is thought they travelled through the centre of the continent from western Africa. In this migration, lasting many centuries, they brought with them the secrets of fashioning iron and making pottery. Like the Wambo, the Damara tribe regard fire as sacred — and believe in one god. They coexist with the Nama and San Bushmen who have lived there from the dawn of time: long before the Damara moved there at least 3,000 years ago. But while the Damara speak the "click" language of the Nama and hunter-gatherer Bushmen, in all other aspects they are Bantu.

These industrious people practise hunting and gathering, pastoralism and even trading. They act as middlemen between the Wambo and the Herero. Some historians maintain that in the past the Damara were enslaved by the Nama. But no matter from which external influences they have benefited, the Damara have certainly retained a great degree of their ethnic cohesion and homogeneity.

From Henties Bay a road cuts east across the Namib. It slices through the dramatic rock landscapes of Damaraland to Spitzkoppe, the Matterhorn of Africa. Its 1,784-metre peak thrusts sheer into the startling blue of the African sky. Beyond this stunning mass of mountain is the small highland farm of Ameib. Nearby, an overhanging rock discloses the site of another national monument: Phillips Cave — famous for its rock painting of a giant white elephant overpainted with a more recent depiction of an antelope.

Another road leads north-east from Henties Bay to a treasury of rock formations and rock art, in and around the 2,574-metre Brandberg massif, Namibia's highest peak. There, amid the bizarre rock formations, German surveyor Reinard Maack discovered the White Lady rock painting in 1918. At first experts thought it Mediterranean in origin because the style was similar to Cretan. Now it's believed the White Lady and other rock paintings in the mighty Brandberg were executed more than 15,000 years ago by ancient San artists.

Some kilometres north of Brandberg, rising out of the desert plains, a red-

brown ridge of hills catches the rays of the westering sun to form the Burnt Mountain, *Verbrandeberg*. In the moments before twilight each evening, Damaraland's constellations of stone seem to take on life. In a deep canyon close by the Burnt Mountain spectacular formations of dolerite rise up from the floor. The fascinating and unusual slabs of rock are known as the Organ Pipes. Just a short distance north-west, Twyfelfontein, meaning doubtful spring, is perhaps the finest neolithic site ever discovered. The jumble of stones contain what may well be Africa's greatest collection of rock engravings. Chiselled into the smooth surfaces of warm stone, the Stone Age illustrations show many species of wildlife.

Above: Late afternoon light bathes this unusual formation of ancient dolerite rocks known as the Organ Pipes near Damaraland's Burnt Mountain.

There are more than 2,000 of them and it is easy to pick out the creatures including rhino, giraffe, elephant, lion, kudu, oryx and ostrich. Spoors are also engraved, but the mystic purpose of these pictures defies explanation. Some maintain the creatures, many seemingly mythical, are for decoration. Yet others

Above: Rhino and giraffe are easily identified in a montage of wildlife rock engravings executed thousands of years ago by prehistoric artists at Twyfelfontein, one of southern Africa's richest repositories of ancient art.

postulate that the designs were etched to show the next animal to fall in a hunt.

North of there the Petrified Forest sprawls across two-and-a-half square kilometres. It is thought to be more than 200 million years old. The great 30-metre tree trunks pose a riddle for they are without branches or roots. Many think they were swept to this spot by floodwaters. Khorixas, the capital of Damaraland, lies between the Ugab and Huab rivers, east of the Petrified Forest. West of the Petrified Forest, the mouth of the Ugab River marks the southern boundary of the infamous Skeleton Coast, one of the world's most treacherous and barren shorelines, where scores of ships and mariners have met their end.

Its gateway dominated by an eerie giant skull and crossbones, the Skeleton Coast Park, established in 1971, is one of Africa's most inaccessible nature reserves. No wider than fifty kilometres at any point, the Skeleton Coast extends north from Cape Cross for approximately 600 kilometres to the Kunene River; with the western sections of Kunene and Erongo — formerly Kaokoland and

Damaraland — forming its hinterland. Before the countless wrecks of ships and skeletons of sailors along its shores gave rise to the macabre name 'Skeleton Coast', it was referred to as the Kaokoveld coast.

Diego Cão was perhaps the coast's first recorded victim. For soon after planting his *padrão* at Cape Cross, and sailing on the return journey to Portugal, Diego Cão died, his mission unfulfilled.

The Benguela Current, with its lethal tidal rips, dense, ghostly fogs and fierce storms, has piled countless ships onto the unforgiving reefs. No one knows for certain just how many vessels have been wrecked, but their skeletons pepper the coast, reaching eerily out of the water, a reminder to others of impending hazards. The coast's dense sea fogs can cover everything in an instant, reducing visibility to virtually nil. Combined with gale-force winds that build mountainous waves, the treacherous reefs of coastal rocks, unexpected shoals and sandbanks — that reach into the sea — make the Skeleton Coast a navigator's nightmare. Debris from their wrecked hulls litters the beaches. Only odd fragments — a porthole crafted in fine brass, a door-handle, chains thick with rust — are recognisable. Over the years, as they slowly change appearance, shift position and disappear, other wrecks take their place.

During 1894 and 1900, Dr George Hartmann, a German geologist with the South West Africa Company, undertook several surveys of the Skeleton Coast — the most extensive of which was in 1896. His aim was to find possible places to establish a harbour and to investigate the occurrence of guano deposits.

Lawrence G. Green, author and traveller, also visited Kaokoveld and the Skeleton Coast in the early 1950s, with what became known as the Carp expedition and wrote about his adventures in *Lords of the Last Frontier*.

In 1954 the idea of a harbour on the north coast arose again, with a view to developing Namibia's fishing industry in the north. For the first time the coastline from Swakopmund to the Kunene River was explored in motor vehicles. The trip, which was completed in twelve days, became known as the Van Zyl expedition.

The creation of the Skeleton Coast Park dates back to 1963 when, mainly for political reasons, the narrow tract of coastline was set aside as a future nature reserve. Since the park was formally proclaimed in 1971 it has been managed as a wilderness reserve — keeping development to a minimum and limiting public access. There lie the wrecks of centuries — the sand and wind-blasted remains of tugs, liners, galleons, clippers, gunboats and trawlers, and their pitiful flotsam and jetsam. The bleached bones of countless whales from the heyday of the whaling fleets lie scattered among the wreckage on the desolate beaches while in tangled heaps at the river mouths are the skeletons of trees, washed down from the interior by the floods of many seasons past.

To roam the bleak shores — where hundreds of bottles lie half-buried, their

Above: Late afternoon sun casts fascinating shadows over the "White Temples", fascinating clay formations left by silt deposits when the Hoarusib River was dammed by the dunes thousands of years ago.

Opposite top: In the middle of the day, the Aporosaura anchietae *lizard does a foot-lifting dance to escape the heat of the sand.*

Opposite: Male tenebrionid beetle shades his mate.

surfaces buffed by wind and wave — is to get a taste of how it might have felt to be marooned on this malicious coast. The few survivors who managed to reach dry land had the odds stacked against them. Until recent times death by dehydration or hunger in the inhospitable Namib was a certainty, for the great rivers which have cut westwards over thousands of years are normally dry. And even when in spate they are blocked by the desert dunes and seldom reach the Atlantic. Nonetheless, their dry channels serve as desert highways for Bushmen and rescue parties.

The Skeleton Coast's best-known wreck is that of the *Dunedin Star.* This British cargo liner of 13,000 tonnes ran aground some kilometres off the shore about forty kilometres south of the Kunene mouth, late on the night of 29 November 1942. On board were twenty-one passengers, a crew of eighty-five, a consignment of mail, and ammunition consisting mainly of explosives.

On the morning of 30 November the captain decided to abandon ship. But the

only motor-boat was rendered useless after three trips, during the course of which all the passengers and forty-two crew were taken ashore. The remaining crew were taken off the *Dunedin Star* by volunteers of the *Téméraire*, transferred safely aboard the *Manchester Division*, and put ashore at Walvis Bay.

Fifty years later, the wreck has been all but washed away by the ceaseless pounding of the breakers but the memory of the drama remains vivid. As well as land vehicles, other ships and an airforce plane were involved in the rescue, including a tug which also ran aground while attempting to haul the stranded ship off the sandbank. A Ventura bomber, which landed onshore to airlift the survivors out, was so bogged down it took four days to dig it out — only for it to crash into the sea after take-off. Searching for water, the castaways came across a grim reminder of their possible fate when they unearthed nine headless skeletons. At the end of the saga, two lives were lost and the last survivor did not reach Windhoek until twenty-six days after the ship ran aground.

Above: Retreating waters expose wreck of one of the countless ships which foundered on Namibia's infamous Skeleton Coast, the world's most notorious shore.

Top: Orange spotted beetle picked out against the stark background of white desert flower.

Above: Softly shaded desert edelweiss clings to desert floor.

Over the centuries, Cape cormorants, often found perched atop the masts and rusting wrecks, have produced a valuable by-product, guano, which lured many early explorers to the infamous Skeleton Coast. Legends of chests filled with gems, and diamonds blanketing the seaboard's shores, were other baits that seduced adventurers and prospectors to their almost certain death. But these fables of untold riches were grossly over-exaggerated. The Skeleton Coast's diamond deposits are modest. The only ones of any note contain the high-quality stones found around Terrace Bay north of the Uniab River. The rusting remains of oil drills and prospecting equipment that pepper the hinterland are pathetic reminders of the prospectors who looked for other riches and failed. As well as diamonds, garnets and an assortment of metals have been located in the area.

Although the Skeleton Coast has subsequently become more accessible as a result of modern technology, from time to time the elements still gain the upper hand. In December 1976, on her maiden voyage, the *Suiderkus*, equipped with the most up-to-date navigational equipment, ran onto the rocks at Möwe Bay. And on land, no matter how well-equipped and technically advanced, the danger of a four wheel-drive vehicle becoming bogged down, whether on the beach, in a river-bed or a brine-pan, is ever present.

It is one reason why the Skeleton Coast Park is managed as a wilderness area. Another is that, inevitably, overexposure of such a fragile ecological system will be detrimental to its existence.

Tourism in the south of the park is restricted to two angling resorts with access either along a coastal route or from the interior. Torra Bay, a camping site, and Terrace Bay, a small self-contained rest-camp, have boundaries within which visitors must remain.

The north of the park may only be visited by fly-in safari, undertaken by a private tour operator who has a concession. Visitors are accommodated in rustic camps and taken around by expert guides in four-wheel drive vehicles. From the air, the Skeleton Coast is an exposed landscape. Its diversity of colour, texture and form, is uncluttered by vegetation or development — much the same as it was a thousand, or perhaps even a million years ago. As perspectives take on new dimensions, horizons expand into infinity and a sense of timelessness pervades.

The oldest rocks on the Skeleton Coast are part of the Damara sequence, deposited between 1,000 and 700 million years ago. Today the granites — molten rock which crystallised deep within the bowels of the earth — are clearly visible at Möwe Bay in a striking mosaic of grey, sectioned by darker grey and pink felspar gravels.

In younger, Mesozoic times, about 170 to 120 million years ago, when the supercontinent of the southern hemisphere, Gondwanaland, began to break apart, deep fissures opened in the crust of the earth — squeezing out vast quantities of lava — which spread like a large flat cake over the Namib platform. Within the brick-red, brown, grey and black lavas lay precious and semi-precious gemstones. These included agate, carnelian, jasper, moss agate and amethyst, the latter found in several layers of large hollow geodes. Amethysts were once mined at Sarusas, but although the quality was high, mining was unprofitable because of high costs and limited demand.

Alluvial diamonds occur sporadically in marine terraces at several locations along the coast. Although of good quality, they are generally small. Because they occur only in small pockets mining them is not viable. Garnets are also found at the Skeleton Coast, usually in the same locations as diamonds, while fine garnet sand covers long stretches of beach in washes of dark maroon. Blown into sandy areas, the sand forms a colourful coating on the back of dunes, creating intriguing patterns on the slipfaces. Tiny black particles of magnetite and ilmenite add to the colourful, surreal patterns characteristically seen on the backs of these dunes, which are a living and integral part of the Skeleton Coast. They are formed by sand deposits churned onto the beaches by Atlantic waves which are then seized by the prevailing south and south-west winds.

One of the most captivating dune formations is the barchan, a crescent-shaped dune which occurs where sand is relatively scarce. Formed and driven by the prevailing south-west wind, these dunes move about three metres a year in a north-easterly direction. The larger barchan dunes roar and rumble when the crest slides down the slipface. The warmer and drier the dune, the more likely it will roar, and the larger the dune, the greater the roar.

Shrub-coppice or hump dunes, a familiar sight, especially near the coast and in dry river courses, in effect, are mounds of sand which have accumulated around vegetation. They are relatively small, averaging up to one or two metres high.

Inland, the Skeleton Coast Park is rich in wildlife, hosting majestic creatures such as giraffe, elephant, lion and black rhino. Although usually dry, the water courses of the Namib have linear oases and considerable underground water. Intermittent natural rock barricades, descending deep into the ground, force the water to the surface where it forms waterholes. But rugged and rocky though the landscape is, and hardy though the creatures are, the Skeleton Coast's ecosystem is extremely vulnerable.

Perhaps the most remarkable physical phenomena are the Namib's many lichens. Prehistoric in origin, more than 100 species cover complete expanses of the Namib's gypsum flats and rocky outcrops. These intriguing organisms, which range widely in colour and form, consist of a fungus and an alga, an association which is considered to be symbiotic. In another strange symbiosis

Above: The rugged red rocks of the Skeleton Coast paint a sombre picture as night draws near.

Opposite top: Cheerful smile reflects the lively outlook of this Himba girl.

Opposite: Pastoral scene in Himba country belies the country's desert image.

between sea and desert, the lichens draw water from the regular fog which haunts the area.

This is a fragile region where footprints and car tracks leave their mark for a thousand years. The unique lichens of the harder gravel plains are so sensitive that they suffer irrevocable damage from careless visitors who, all too often, roam the park in ignorance.

The gravel plains are also home to the rare and diminishing Damara tern which lays its eggs in open nests on the plains. That they and other outstanding features of this incomparable wilderness still survive is testimony to the dedication of a handful of people who work tirelessly to preserve a rich natural heritage.

These beguiling plains extend into Damaraland, epitomizing the beauty of Namibia and the hypnotic spell Africa casts on visitors and residents alike. In *Venture to the Interior*, Laurens van der Post notes: '. . . the truth was that Africa

was with me whether I came back or not. For years it had stood apart from me: a dark, unanswered, implacable question in my life. It was that no longer. I felt that I was not leaving it, but taking it with me.'

Above: Early morning fog which descends over the Namib Desert supplies both flora and fauna with just enough moisture to survive, in this, the oldest desert on earth.

Because of the region's isolation, only recently has it been touched by the twentieth century. But, as evidenced by the surprising number of Stone Age axes and tools, and the extraordinary rock engravings that have been discovered, it has been occupied for thousands of years. The discovery of seashells and fish bones far inland indicates that various hunter-gatherer communities migrated to the interior from the Atlantic seaboard. Then, in the last 200 years, European colonialists forced many other cultural groups northwards off their fertile ancestral plains into these badlands where they now eke out a frugal existence.

Among the largest groups of the Kaokoveld are the Himba in the north and the Herero in the south. But throughout the last four centuries the dominant

Above: Marine wreckage underlines the menace of Namibia's Skeleton Coast.

group has been the Herero. The land and the rivers both take their name from the tribe which migrated there from Angola during the sixteenth century. They also flooded into Owambo to graze their livestock in the Etosha Pan but were forced westwards by the warlike response of the Wambo. Some 200 years later, around the middle of the eighteenth century, the Kaokoland Herero continued their southward migration to the more hospitable grazing lands of central Namibia. It was a fatal trek. The resident Nama took up arms and almost devastated the tribe, seizing their cattle and reducing the survivors to paupers.

One group, the Tjimba-Herero, fled back to Angola, begging food and shelter from the Ngwambwe people along the way. Himba tribal lore is full of warnings about the Nama and includes cautions not to light big fires, lest the Nama pinpoint their position and plunder their herds. Even now, despite the tourists who flock there and an influx of Western culture, the Himba cling to their traditions — rejecting alien ways of existence. Their scattered settlements, clusters of distinctive thatched, beehive-shaped huts, are fashioned from saplings, usually mopane, and plastered with a mixture of mud and cow dung. Looking down from a plane it is hard to believe that anyone or anything could survive in this barren land at the very edge of existence, where the Himba, who are superb pastoralists, tend a few goats and cattle or craft trinkets for tourists.

Like the Herero, the Himba trace their lineage down through the female side of the family. It follows a rare system of double descent, by which members belong to a patriarchy as well, a system of kinship and ancestry which is astounding in its complexity. The classifications, seemingly endless in their scale and scope, define each kinsman's role, responsibility and path of descent to a degree unthought of in the West.

Scorning the trappings of modern civilization, much in the manner of the Maasai of East Africa, the Himba have become a fascination for Western observers. Fire, which is sacred to the Himba, is used to maintain contact with the spirits of dead ancestors who are rooted in an eternal flame — a common belief of many African peoples. When the community uproots itself to move on to new pastures this hallowed, living flame is carried along. The fires, *okuruwo*, are central to clan celebrations and festivals, and firesticks symbolise the bond between revered ancestors and sacred fire. Associated with the flame are two classes of sacred cattle used as ritual sacrifice.

Events in the early 1980s devastated Himba society forcing them to improvise in ways which were perhaps unthinkable to previous generations. During three years without rain, which claimed more than eighty per cent of their cattle, the Himba were left with only their animal skins to chew for nourishment. International aid thrust them into closer contact with the modern world. Driven from their homeland by famine, many stumbled into prostitution and despair.

Now, as an elder strikes a match, he waits a moment, hoping the ancestors will understand, before rekindling the sacred fire. For the Himba are in open confrontation with the forces of the twentieth century with the choice of conforming or resisting its influence. Ironically, the only certainty is that whatever they choose will inevitably signal the end of their extraordinarily rich cultural heritage. As they struggle to preserve their ageless lifestyle the Himba can do little more than move deeper into the remote corners of the Kaokoveld, there to share an austere existence with migrant groups such as the Tjavikwa, Ngwambwe, Ngumbi and Kuvare, from southern Angola.

Kaokoland's animals and plants flourish because they have become fine-tuned to their environment over thousands of years. For each creature there are just enough plants to eat and for each plant just enough water. On the dry river-bed or rolling sand dunes, on granite plains or between ocean and shore, each creature has found a special niche.

The Skeleton Coast is very much a product of the dense coastal fogs and cold

Above: Last resting place of a denizen of the deep, washed ashore at Cape Frio.

Above: Bird's eye view of half buried ship submerged on the southern shores of Skeleton Coast.

sea breezes caused by the icy Benguela Current and the hot bergwinds from the interior. These foster both its singular ecosystem and its aura of mystery and impenetrability. Yet contrary to popular belief the coast is relatively cool with temperatures rarely exceeding 30°C.

Paradoxically, although the Namib Desert has one of the most humid atmospheres in the world, the layer of moist air is so thin it does not contain enough moisture for rain. While temperatures inland rise sharply during the day, the coast itself remains cool throughout the year, except on those winter days when bergwinds blow to make it warmer than in summer.

The south and south-west winds persist throughout the year, while the infamous *Ostwind*, a typical bergwind, blows from April to July. It brings life-giving detritus from the interior as food for the many small and uniquely adapted creatures of the dunes.

One of the most remarkable of these is the trapdoor spider, also known as the dancing white lady spider. These large white hunting spiders perform a curious ballet — reminiscent of a line of high-kicking vaudeville chorus girls — when alarmed. They build their home by digging a hole in the sand, covering the walls with a cobweb lining and constructing a kind of trapdoor over the opening. When laden with eggs the female is twice as heavy as the male which she needs for fertilization, but when the deed is done the damsel delivers the kiss of death. These spiders are so powerful that they often kill large geckos. But black dune wasps prey on the spiders. When threatened, the spider forms itself into a tight ball and rolls rapidly down a dune slope to escape. Clusters of up to eighty eggs at a time are laid in a silk cocoon and hatch within a fortnight. The mother feeds the voracious youngsters for two months before leaving them to their destiny. Competition between them is so fierce that only about ten per cent survive.

Top: Ghost crab in threatening mood.

In Kaokoland there are nine endemic species of bird, the endemic black-faced impala, and at least one endemic lizard — along with rhino, lion, giraffe and elephant. Black rhino, another of Africa's great pachyderms, were once abundant throughout Damaraland and Kaokoland but they, too, have been brought to the edge of extinction by poaching and hunting. Now only a handful of these elusive creatures wander the dry water courses of the Kaokoveld. It is there that lion also lie in ambush at waterholes for gemsbok and springbok. Other creatures found in the wilderness of Kaokoland include giraffe, genet, mountain zebra, brown hyena, ostrich and baboon, springbok and gemsbok. Many come down into the desert from the mountains and plains when the rains fall and the rivers flow.

Only rarely in flood, the river-beds provide migration routes for the region's desert-adapted elephants. The creature has become the emblematic animal of the Namibia Nature Foundation. Established in the late 1980s, the Foundation is concerned not only with the conservation of the desert elephant, imperilled black rhino and Cape vulture, but less publicised habitats and animals, such as those of Namibia's rare wetlands: crocodile, hippo and marsh-dwelling antelopes, the sitatunga and lechwe, as well as the threatened Damara tern, wild dog and natural wonders such as the Namib's vast lichen fields. The Foundation has fifteen trustees and the founding chairman was Namibia's Chief Justice.

Few sights are more thrilling than those of a desert elephant roaming the Namib wilderness in solitude. In rare moments they can be seen forging down the dunes, running and sliding in an explosion of sand. It indicates the extent to which they have adapted to this inhospitable environment. Ancient rock engravings and the records of explorers indicate that they were once widespread in Namibia. In the last few decades the migration route between the Namib and Etosha has been cut by the development of tribal homelands and

Above: Stark beauty of the majestic landscape of sand and rock near Sarusas.

farms. There are calls to re-establish the corridor to allow the elephants to move freely between these two crucial natural reserves.

The Namib elephants are endowed with a prodigious thirst and cover as much as sixty kilometres a day in search of the 200 litres or more of water they need each day to sustain them. Elephants have an uncanny knack of finding water. In times of great drought they use their tusks to dig deep into a dry river bed. Shattered tusks are witness to the tragic failures. But their waterholes serve a multitude of other wild and wonderful creatures, great and small, in a vivid example of interdependence. Poachers and drought ravaged southern Africa during the 1980s and almost undid efforts to conserve the Kaokoveld's elephant herds. Yet they are essential to the balance of the Namib's ecosystem. Beside making waterholes for other creatures, they also propagate plants. Their digestive systems break down the outer coating of a seed and allow it to germinate when it passes out through their dung.

Above: Desert flower in a blaze of yellow.

Another vital participant in this process is the ubiquitous dung beetle. They arrive swiftly and in great numbers to clean up the wake of the great pachyderms. The ancient Egyptians likened these scarabs, rolling their balls of dung across the landscape, to the mysterious force causing the sun to circle across the sky. Dung beetles don't just clean up animal waste, particularly elephant droppings — far more efficiently than the modern technological processes of urban society — they also recycle life-giving nutrients like nitrogen, aerate soil through their burrowing, and generally improve and cultivate the environment. In the Namib, or among the great elephant pastures by the Okavango and in the Caprivi Strip, these insects reduce elephant dung balls to plant fibre in as little as an hour.

The animals that live in the dry river-beds are not necessarily typical desert fauna. They have regular access to water, and feed on vegetation that also occurs in the interior. The larger species — such as black rhino and lion — are

migratory. They move up and down the river courses, often increasing in numbers when food becomes scarce in the interior. Giraffe are also occasionally seen there as well as chacma baboons. Smaller animals which occur commonly are Cape hare, the crested porcupine, genet, caracal and the African wild cat. Larger mammals seen most commonly on the plains are springbok and gemsbok. In years when good rain-showers occur and there is sufficient grass cover, their numbers increase. Even zebra move in from the interior, followed by beasts of prey such as hyena, lion and leopard.

An impressive bird sometimes seen in the river courses is the lappet-faced vulture, which nests on the tops of large acacia trees. Smaller birds commonly seen are Cape sparrows, mountain chats, bokmakieries, titbabblers, red-eyed bulbuls and mousebirds. Several species, such as Egyptian geese, avocets, red-knobbed coots and Cape teals, are found at the waterholes.

Most numerous of the coastal birds are Cape cormorants and gulls, while small flocks of the rare Damara tern are a familiar sight. Coastal lagoons and waterholes are frequented by lesser and greater flamingos. While another colony of about 50,000 Cape fur seals occurs further north at Cape Frio.

The sand dunes at the Skeleton Coast play host to unusual and highly specialised dune-dwellers. These include termites, beetles, fish moths and ants, which are preyed on by lizards, snakes, spiders, crickets, flies, scorpions, chameleons and wasps.

Other scavengers are the ghost crabs, fair-weather creatures which live under the surface along the beaches, emerging when the sand is warmed by the sun. At the slightest provocation they scuttle frenetically towards the sea, sometimes in large squadrons.

Unique to the northern Namib are the 'white' tenebrionid beetles, which are able to remain active on the dune surface long after their black relatives have dived under the sand to avoid overheating.

On closer inspection an apparently smooth dune slipface reveals an intricate network of many different tracks. Those of the sidewinding adder, a diagonal series of broken transverse lines, are distinctive. The sidewinder drinks by sucking droplets of condensed moisture from its body. It takes refuge in the sand during the daytime, lying with only its eyes above the surface.

An interesting lizard found in the dunes is the colourful, translucent Palmatogecko. Exclusively nocturnal and ethereal in appearance, it has a salmon pink and white body, large, dark protruding eyes, white lids and turquoise blue spots on the head. The large vegetarian sand-diving Skoogi lizard, endemic to the northern Namib, is characterised by its glossy orange and creamy yellow skin, the male having a shiny black chin and throat. The shovel-nosed lizard, with its delicate mother-of-pearl sheen, is smaller. When temperatures are high these lizards perform a shuffling footlifting dance, holding the tail above the

Top: Cattle egret enjoying a much-needed drink.

Above: Black-faced finch takes a snack.

Opposite: Sobering reminder of the precarious desert lifestyle, skull and horns of oryx.

surface of the dune, to keep cool. If disturbed they dive beneath the sand with a rapid cork-screw movement.

The dense belt of fog which hangs over the ocean near the coast on most days is pushed between forty and fifty kilometres inland creating a relatively cool and moist zone all along the coast. Such a regular inflow of moisture has created an extraordinary plant community with a large number of endemic species. Subjected to extremes of temperature, strong winds and encroaching sands, these plants ensured their survival by developing a wide spectrum of ingenious adaptations to acquire, retain and store moisture.

Some of the most curious plants grow on the mountain slopes. Examples of these are the strange hedgehog-like elephant's foot, which anchors itself with its long taproot in among the rocks; the conspicuous *hoodia*, with its large, reddish-brown plate-like flowers; the small well-camouflaged *trichocaulon*, which spreads flat on the ground with knobbly, finger-like leaves; and the Bushman's candle, with its pink and white flowers and resin-like bark which can be burnt as incense. Truly outlandish are the stunted low-spreading *commiphora* trees with their thick swollen stems.

Vegetation which grows in association with dunes is widely distributed throughout the Skeleton Coast. Common examples are the ganna or brackbush, narra, dollar-bush, desert parsley and dune lucerne. Although these bushes appear to grow on top of the dunes, the dunes, in fact, develop or 'grow' around the bush, which remains on top by extending its root system.

Ganna in particular, despite its nondescript appearance, provides valuable fodder for the animals of the desert. Springbok, gemsbok, ostrich and many other birds, as well as insects, feed off its highly nutritious dusky grey-green leaves.

Another plant that traps sand is the narra. It holds together much bigger dunes than the ganna bushes, drawing water from rare underground reservoirs. Endemic to the Namib, it has thorns but no leaves. The round, prickly fruit is eaten by a variety of creatures, including gemsbok and hyena. It is also prized by the people of the Namib. They pulp the seed to make a kind of cake, and ferment its watery sap to make beer.

Two common species of euphorbia occur — the plains euphorbia, which grows in flat areas, and the cactus-like candelabra euphorbia, growing on rocky hills and mountains.

Seeds of other interesting plants are carried from the interior and grow into trees and shrubs in the dry river-beds. They tap down into the water below, and are essential browsing for giraffe, elephants and rhino. Some are remarkably big and their roots so strong and deep they survive the rare seasons when the rivers become torrents, and threaten to tear their hold from the banks. One, the leadwood tree, is sacred to the Herero, who revere it as the tree of life from

Below: When conditions permit, Namibia is a profusion of floral colour.

which they sprang. The wood, which is covered with smooth grey bark, is heavier than water, and its roots spread out hundreds of feet along the dry river-beds in search of water. Its gnarled, contorted shape fascinates all those who come across it, as C. J. Andersson notes in *The Okavango River.*

My name is Omborombonga,
I flourish south of Ondonga
(The country of agricultural Ovambo)
My land of birth is that of the pastoral Herero
(Better known as the race
Called Cattle Damaras),
Who claim me as their Ma and Pa
And sure I do not know what a';
To me this 's strange and odd
For I yield nothing but wood.
But why blame people's fancy?—
Their parent I am and must be.

Major components of the character and ecology of the Skeleton Coast are the rivers that drain westwards towards the sea. These rivers also carry plant forms, normally foreign to an arid environment, from the interior into the desert. Such comparatively rich vegetation, sustained by subterranean water, supports a wide spectrum of animal life, including large and small mammals, birds, reptiles and insects.

Transverse rock barriers force some of the water to the surface, thereby creating permanent and semi-permanent waterholes and the so-called *gorras*, sand-holes under the surface. These contain water and are dug open by elephant and gemsbok.

The largest river is the Hoarusib, which comes down in flood at least once a year. The Hoanib, Huab, Khumib, Koichab, Uniab and Ugab Rivers reach the sea from time to time, while the Sechomib, Nadas, Munutum and Odondojengo flow rarely and, when they do, peter out in sand.

The Hoarusib starts its journey westwards from the Otjihipa and Etorocha Mountains in the highlands of Kaokoland in dramatic fashion, twisting through a narrow gorge. As it plunges down to sea through a spectacular array of scenery, the river cuts through a canyon dominated by incredible castles of clay, known as "White Temples".

Composed of yellow-white clay that crumbles at a touch, these eroded pinnacles, each with its own distinctive shape, were formed from the silt deposits of this once-mighty waterway. Perched high above the river banks, they are reminiscent of the ancient fortresses and palaces of the Middle East. One or two even suggest the pyramids of old Egypt. Juxtaposed in front of the

Above: The fast flowing Kunene River provides the border between Namibia and Angola in the remote and little-visited Hartmann mountains.

sheer wall of the canyon, they have a startling, almost supernatural quality. They are thought by geomorphologists to be the result of the damming of the river by the dunes within the last 100,000 years.

Central to the northern region is Owambo — newly named Omusati, Oshana, Ohangwena and Ojikoto — home of the Wambo, a cultural group formed by eight distinct sub-groups, totalling up to 800,000. These proud people are spread out over Namibia's vast north-west savannah. With its luxuriant vegetation, watered by many rivers and abundant rainfall, Owambo is lush contrast to the stark aridity of the Namib and Kalahari. This land, where drought was almost unknown until recently, yields a rich harvest of maize, millet and other cereals, pumpkins and other vegetables, melons and other fruit. Besides tilling the land and planting, the Wambo fish their rivers for barbel with traditional wicker nets.

The Wambo's extended, matrilineal families live in stockaded compounds in beehive-shaped mud and wood huts. These dwellings have separate pens for

livestock and grain stores under the same thatched roof. When Wambo society came into contact with the Europeans in the mid-nineteenth century their lifestyle was changed irrevocably. Ancient rituals, centred around a sacred fire, were abandoned in favour of Christianity introduced by missionaries. But from time immemorial the Wambo believed in one God, the supreme creator.

Above: Rocks sculpted by the Kunene River have produced ethereal shapes along the water's edge.

Approximately 400,000 people — thirty-five per cent of Namibia's population — live in the flat, sandy floodplain area of central Owambo. They are dependent for their livelihood on flood-waters which sometimes occur in the oshanas, the interconnected drainage channels that flow in the area.

The floods result in a flush of grass that supports the many cattle, goats and donkeys, and bring in frogs and fish that contribute valuable protein to the diet. The nutritious drought-resistant cereal, pearly millet, *mahangu*, is cultivated there. The environment is currently threatened by overgrazing and deforestation, as well as by roads and canals, which obstruct water-flow in the oshanas.

Below: Colourful lichens cling to a rock in Kaokoveld.

Bottom: Hirpicium gazenioides, *or desert daisy, endure the full glare of the midday sun.*

At the northern edge of Owambo the Kunene River plunges over the Ruacana Falls in a foaming, crystal-white column of water. Some kilometres westward, as it races through the Baynes Mountain, along the Namibian-Angola border, it takes yet another leap towards the Atlantic over the Epupa Falls. Then it cuts through the remote Otjihipa and Hartmann Mountains into the ocean. Lush riverine forest coats its banks with a cloak of verdure and its waters teem with crocodiles. But the great numbers of wildlife — elephant, hippo, rhino and impala — that once roamed along its course were almost wiped out early this century. Where the river's estuary empties into the Atlantic, the crocodile, a species that has endured through 130 million years, is joined by one of the marine world's most antediluvian creatures, the leather-backed turtle, which swarms there to breed. Many species of fish, including the fighting tiger fish, leather fish and springers, flourish in the Kunene's fast-flowing water. The potent power has not gone unnoticed, however, and the waters are being harnessed by a hydroelectric development which, when complete, will provide half of the country's entire energy needs.

But until recently the river's existence was shrouded in myth and legend and western observers doubted its existence. C. J. Andersson noted in his 1856 book *Lake Ngami*: 'Many years previously to our visit to the Ovambo, a French frigate discovered the embouchure of a magnificent river, known as the Cunene, between the seventeenth and eighteenth degrees of south latitude. Other vessels were sent out to explore it, and to ascertain its course, but, strange to say, they searched in vain for it!'

6 · DRY

RIVERS, DESERT LAGOONS

Previous pages: Springbok and zebra quench their thirst beneath a cloudless Namibian sky at one of Etosha National Park's perennial waterholes.

On the plains in the far north of Namibia, a tract of shimmering haze denotes the dry bed of a once vast lake. Each year, at the height of the rains, it fills again to become an inland sea. And there, at Etosha, the Great White Place of Dry Water, this *Journey through Namibia* reaches its climax.

Covering more than 22,000 square kilometres, Etosha's unending wilderness is a cradle of wildlife that is home to many animals, insects, reptiles, plants and birds. At its heart lies the Etosha Pan, once a large lake covering more than 6,000 square kilometres, until an uplifting of the southern African plain twelve million years ago tilted the landscape and caused the Kunene River to flow westward. The first description of Etosha is by C. J. Andersson in *Lake Ngami*.

> 'In the course of the first day's journey, we traversed an immense hollow, called Etosha, covered with saline encrustations, and having wooded and well-defined borders. Such places are in Africa designated salt-pans. The surface consisted of a soft, greenish-yellow, clay soil, strewed with fragments of small sand-stone, of a purple tint. Strange to relate, we had scarcely been ten minutes on this ground, when the lower extremities of ourselves and cattle became of the same purple colour. In some rainy seasons, the Ovambo informed us, the locality was flooded, and had all the appearance of a lake; but now it was quite dry, and the soil strongly impregnated with salt. Indeed, close in shore, this commodity was to be had of a pure quality.'

Above: Capricious ground squirrel forages for seeds and nuts in Etosha's scorched wilderness.

Andersson and Francis Galton, a cousin of Charles Darwin, camped on an Owambo grazing ground called Strong Waters, now Namutoni, at the eastern edge of Etosha.

> 'At Omutjamatunda, there is a most copious fountain, situated on some rising ground, and commanding a splendid prospect of the surrounding country. It was a refreshing sight to stand on the borders of the fountain, which was luxuriously over-grown with towering reeds, and sweep with the eye the extensive plain encircling the base of the hill; frequented as it was, not only by vast herds of domesticated cattle, but with the lively springbok and troops of striped zebras. If the monotony of our dreary wanderings had not thus been relieved, I do not know how we should have borne up against our constant trials and difficulties.'

Many more explorers journeyed to Etosha in the second half of the nineteenth century, all recording its abundance of wildlife. Finally a group of Boer settlers, the Dorsland Trekkers from the Transvaal, travelled through the Kalahari to Damaraland and Etosha.

One group, which stayed for two years at the site of the small town of Rietfontein, was led there by Gert Alberts. Some small ruins, and a memorial to Alberts' wife, commemorate their stay. Eventually, the pioneers teamed up

Opposite: Nature has given the giraffe, the world's tallest creature, a complex system of valves and reservoirs to maintain blood pressure even when it stoops to drink.

Above: Fortress turned hotel — gleaming white Namutoni Game Lodge in Etosha National Park, once a lonely and vulnerable outpost of German colonial power.

with another group and travelled on to Etosha, spending some time at Namutoni before moving to southern Angola.

Just after the turn of the century, in 1902, the Germans built a small fortress near the fountain at Namutoni. Made from unfired clay bricks, the rectangular stronghold had towers at each corner. In 1904, the small outpost was razed by Herero and Owambo warriors after the garrison had fled. It was rebuilt after the Herero were put down and restored and renovated in 1957. This Beau Geste-style fortress is now a national monument and a game lodge. At sundown each evening a lone bugler sounds the Last Post from the top of the gleaming white walls of the north-east tower. And, as the shadows inexorably lengthen and day melts into sultry African night, the flag of free Namibia that flutters over the fortress is gently lowered.

The colonists decimated South West Africa's wildlife early this century with complete disregard for many species. Fortunately for Etosha, in 1907 the

Above: Oryx wax fat on Etosha National Park's sparse summer pastures. In profile these sleek animals appear to have only one horn and gave rise to the legend of the unicorn.

Governor, Dr. F. von Lindequist, divided a vast area surrounding it into three game reserves. The second of these reserves, which encompassed Etosha Pan and much of the Kaokoveld, between the Kunene River and Hoarusib River, covered 93,240 square kilometres. In 1947, however, its size shrank dramatically. Large sections of Kaokoland were given back to the Herero for living space, while 3,406 square kilometres were sliced out of the Etosha wilderness, only for them to be restored nine years later by the so-called 'Elephant Commission'.

In 1963, the reserve was cut to a third of its size — a calamitous blow to the ecosystem which left Etosha devastated. Many rare and endangered species had to be relocated. Soon after, when Etosha was gripped by an unrelenting drought that lasted years, the wound became critical. The last two decades before independence were a mixture of misfortune and blessing for Etosha and its animals. At prohibitive cost, the park was fenced during 1973 to reduce

Above: Burchell's zebra with foal in Etosha National Park.

poaching. But it severed the ancient migration trails of the park's elephant herds and made Etosha a closed unit, a vast safari park with captive creatures suddenly robbed of their seasonal movements in search of water and food. Confined within the park, the animals were under threat from disease, as well as lack of water and shortage of pasture. Infections like anthrax, rabies, rinderpest and bovine pneumonia can spread all too swiftly, annihilating whole populations, when migratory herds are no longer able to move out of infected areas.

Zoologists fear that when the park management fenced in the animals they also fenced in an entire range of killer diseases, like rinderpest, which swept through Etosha's kudu herds in the early 1980s. Another, anthrax, was a particularly vindictive killer in the decades from the 1960s. And even a decade after the crippling drought of the 1980s southern Africa still suffered from lack of water. The creatures most severely affected were great mammals like the

Above: Antediluvian survivor of the African savannah — slow-moving leopard tortoise, one of Namibia's more endearing reptiles.

rhino and elephant. The drought came when the park's elephant population was increasing dramatically. But new management techniques, including sinking boreholes powered by windmills, helped to restore Etosha's health. Radio collars were fitted to some elephants so that their movements could be monitored by satellite.

Now Etosha prospers as an incomparable wildlife retreat where the camera and not the rifle reigns supreme. The southern winter, between May and September, when water is scarce and thousands of animals converge on the perennial springs and waterholes, is the best time for game viewing. There is a wide selection of amenities in the park, ranging from basic to luxury.

Two main roads lead into Etosha, one from Outjo in the south, the other from a junction of the Tsumeb-Ondangwa road in the east. The Outjo road enters the park at Okaukuejo, on the Etosha Pan's south-western periphery, through the Andersson Gate. The camp there was established late in the nineteenth century to control smuggling, poaching and animal diseases. It became the first camp to cater for tourists and is now the largest. Okaukuejo is also the centre for Etosha's Ecological Institute, founded in 1974. The camp overlooks a permanent waterhole which is floodlit at night — giving visitors an insight into the habits of a wide range of nocturnal creatures. Even diurnal creatures graze and splash in the shallows under the light of these artificial moons. The sight of kudu and rhino, their frames mirrored in the black water, is unforgettable. This natural theatre stars large numbers of lion, giraffe, wildebeest and elephant in a nightly drama of the wild.

Seventy kilometres north-east of Okaukuejo, the road to Namutoni cuts through another camp established in the late 1960s. Halali, which lies at the base of a small dolomite hill, takes its name from the custom of German foresters sounding a fanfare at the end of a successful hunt.

Animals seen at the waterholes along the edge of the pan in the vicinity of Halali include wildebeest, zebra and gemsbok. Namutoni is another seventy-five kilometres further on.

Etosha's stark beauty stuns the visitor but its landscapes are far from barren. Besides boreholes, many natural springs filter up through a strata of permeable limestone, their crystal waters providing Etosha with a matchless charm.

At the centre of the park, the 6,000 square kilometres of the pan, which covers about a quarter of Etosha National Park's 22,270 square kilometres, is usually inundated during the summer rains between November and March. Few plants can withstand the alkaline waters — twice as salty as seawater — but they encourage many colourful types of algae and a specialised grass, *Sporobolus salsus*, that thrives in saltwater. It covers a large area of the pan's southern reaches. Away from the pan, savannah grasses cover the flat plains in response to the first flush of rain. The prairies support thousands of plains animals —

Opposite: Snarling face of a young cheetah — the world's fastest land creature — in Etosha National Park, one of their last two strongholds in Africa.

Above: Pride of lionesses shelter from midday heat in an Etosha woodland.

such as zebra, springbok and wildebeest — which thrive on the protein-rich grasses. As summer arrives, these mighty herds move westwards to the Grootvlakte region's lush meadows where acacia thorn trees also offer shade and nourishment.

The mopane is the most common tree, much favoured by the park's elephant herds which rely on its bark, roots, branches and leaves for a great deal of their fodder. With its higher rainfall and deep soils, Etosha's north-east region, the sandveld area, supports many kinds of large tree, while tamboti, *Spirostachys africana,* and terminalia woodlands cover the south-eastern expanses. The shady retreats entice dik-dik, leopard, elephant, giraffe and many more creatures to seek relief from the midday heat. And in the west stand some of Africa's finest and strangest trees, including the outlandish ghost tree, *Moringa ovalifolia.* Its contorted form looks like a smaller, smoother, more polished version of the baobab. Endemic only to Etosha, they form the Haunted Forest, *sprokieswoud,*

Above: Etosha National Park's 2,000 elephants are characterised by their small, mineral-deficient tusks.

situated thirty kilometres west of Okaukuejo. There are also some ghost trees north-west of the Andersson Gate. The trees inspire many legends. The San maintain that after God had created the world, the universe and everything in it, a bunch of moringa trees were left over. Not knowing where to put them, God thrust them root upwards into the wilderness.

In all respects — the creatures that live there, the trees, bushes and flowers, the birds and the insects, even the views — Etosha is a magical place. Nothing matches the miracle of the rains which bring it to life, transforming the landscapes into a profusion of colour and greenery.

In late October the heat becomes oppressive as, day by day, the clouds build until towering thunderheads fill the sky. Finally, early in November, comes the moment when far away on the horizon the sky becomes black and brooding,

Above: For elephant and zebra alike, their search through Etosha's wild, unending expanses is always for edible greenery and water.

blotting out the sun. And then the clouds open and the deluge begins. The speed with which flowers and grasses grow is astonishing. Within hours the baked brown earth is peppered with green shoots. Now the measureless herds move westwards from their winter havens at Halali and Gemsbokvlakte to other regions of Etosha's fastness. During a good year the rains, heaviest early in January, continue into April.

The infrequent torrential downpours sometimes signal the rare appearance of one of Namibia's most remarkable natural curiosities — the giant pyxie, *pyxicephalus adspersus*. Also known as the African bullfrog, this amphibian is one of the largest frogs in the world. These creatures spend as much as ten months, and often years, buried deep beneath the sun-baked plain virtually in suspended animation. And although widespread throughout southern Africa,

Above: Rare, endangered black rhino and calf scurry nervously through Etosha's sere savannah.

few people have ever been lucky enough to see or photograph them. Those who have, recall the occasion with awe.

Wildlife photographers and writers Daryl and Sharna Balfour, whose book *Etosha* was published in 1992, remember vividly the day in the 1990s when they saw these creatures for the first and only time:

> 'There they were, waddling about in their strange, ungainly gait, feeding for perhaps the first time in a year. We stopped our vehicle and watched spellbound as the frogs continued their frenzy . . . . Returning [the next day] . . . we were greeted by a curious "whooop . . . whooop . . . whooop" sound . . . then, everywhere across the countryside, we saw huge, yellowish frogs leaping, splashing and waddling about.'

Although Etosha looks its best in summer, many prefer the winter months. By July, the climate is cool, and the animals are once again congregated about

Top: Ostrich strutting through parched terrain of Etosha National Park.
Above: Yellow-billed hornbill in the shadows that cloak Etosha woodland.

the main waterholes — making game-watching easy. Species common to the park include zebra, wildebeest, lion, cheetah, impala, kudu, elephant, giraffe, springbok. There are also five endangered species — the black rhino, black-faced impala, roan, Hartmann's mountain zebra and the Damaraland dik-dik.

In the arid winter months the park's elephants rid themselves of parasites with dust baths. It is common to see calves rolling about while their elders shower themselves with dust. In the haunting light of summer, caked in silvery mud, these ancient mammals are a spectacular sight. An African elephant may weigh anything between three-and-a-half to six-and-a-half tonnes. It sustains its strength by a prodigious daily intake of water and between ninety and 270 kilos of fodder. Perhaps closest of all animals to mankind in its social structure, the species shares another unique similarity. Elephant and man are thought to be the only creatures which destroy the environment that sustains them. Elephant herds fell woodlands which turn into grasslands. When they ranged freely they would move on after levelling the tree cover. Over the years woodlands would regenerate, then the elephants would return, and the cycle would begin once again. Now, at Etosha, their range is limited by the fence around the wilderness and the land has no time to recover. But the elephants of Etosha seem to have learned the need to care for their environment. They no longer uproot whole trees when they forage for food, but graze selectively by picking at specific branches.

Mankind is also the elephant's greatest enemy in the battle for room to live. Sadly, elephant can only increase its numbers at the expense of man — and vice versa. The confrontation with poachers and expanding rural populations has cost it dear all across Africa.

Elephants depend almost entirely on their trunks for scent, communication, washing and cleaning, carrying and clearing, eating and drinking. Like Namibia's other desert-adapted elephants, the Etosha population have small tusks which are often broken when they quarry down to reach underground water. Mineral deficiencies also cause brittle, stunted tusks.

Life spans are governed by the rate at which the lower teeth are replaced. As one is worn away, the next one moves down the jaw to push it out and take its place. When the last one has come forward and is worn down, at any time between fifty and seventy years of age, the elephant must eventually die of starvation. Although their sight is poor, elephants have an excellent sense of smell and well-tuned hearing. Their brains weigh between three-and-a-half and five kilos — three-and-a-half times as heavy as the human brain.

As the reflection of a full moon ripples across the surface of the Okaukuejo waterhole, the creatures on its bank freeze in sudden fear — listening to a faint noise which has disturbed them. Slowly they relax and vanish into the shadows of night, a small herd of elephants the last to leave.

Above: Angelic though they may appear in flight, the keen eyes of the raptors miss little in the form of edible prey either in the sky or on the ground.

Now enters a single black rhino from one of Africa's largest surviving populations. After sixty-four million years on earth, this creature clings by the last of its highly prized horns to the edge of the abyss of extinction. In the early 1970s Africa had 65,000 black rhinos. Only two decades later, there were fewer than 2,000. About 350 rhino — among them four extremely rare three-horned rhino — roam Etosha's wilderness. With ten per cent of the world population, the park is at the forefront of rhino conservation. But even in Etosha their safety is not guaranteed.

With a kilo of horn worth thousands of dollars, the carnage was further fuelled by: an insatiable appetite for trophies; their favoured fashion in the Arab World as dagger handles; and as medical potions concocted from ground rhino horn. Indeed, poaching reached such levels by 1988 that an anti-poaching unit was formed to challenge gangs armed with modern automatic weapons. The APU's success was swift.

Above: Tawny eagle on the prowl in thorn scrub.

The hook-lipped black rhino of Etosha, smaller than Africa's other species, the white rhino or square-lipped rhino — reintroduced into Namibia's Waterberg Plateau Park — are at last increasing. They are, in fact, a sub-species of the desert rhino, whose distribution once extended as far south as Cape Town's Table Mountain. Now zoologists are collaborating on a plan to reintroduce the Namibian rhino into the Cape Province's northern reaches, and also to relocate them in the safer regions closer to the heart of Etosha.

Radio transmitters inserted at the base of the horn, after the rhino has been drugged, allow rangers to track the movements of these solitary creatures.

Black rhino are smaller than white rhino and both the size and shape of the lips — not colour — distinguish the two. The square-lipped white rhino is so named because it is wide-mouthed and *weit* has been anglicised by misuse. Black rhino weigh from 900 to 1,350 kilos and an average horn varies between fifty and ninety centimetres long.

Above: One of Namibia's most elusive antelopes. Male greater kudu are endowed with magnificent lyrate horns.

Later, before dawn, a solitary giraffe makes its way to the water, scanning nervously around before stooping to drink. This is when they are most vulnerable to predatory lion and leopard. Nature has given the world's tallest creature a complex biology to help it cope with the high life.

A unique system of canals and valves maintains its blood pressure at a constant level — whether standing tall or bending down to drink. Forelegs splayed far apart, the giraffe is a gracious sight as it lowers its head to drink.

Long revered by Namibia's Bushmen, giraffes feature frequently in their ancient rock carvings and tribal lore. One San legend relates how God ordered the giraffe to watch that the sun did not change its course across the sky. God was so pleased with its vigil that as a tribute he made a great giraffe in the sky, which the San use for navigation in the desert. The Bushmen point out the giraffe, *Tutwa*, the constellation which western astronomers know as the Southern Cross.

Above: Oryx turns its back on elephant calf which wallows in a fast-shrinking Etosha waterhole.

More closely related to deer than any other living creature, the giraffe, with its curious lope, maintains a speed of up to fifty-six kilometres an hour. A full-grown giraffe is eighteen feet high and weighs up to 1,270 kilos.

Another San legend tells how the cheetah got its speed. Able to sprint at 115 kilometres an hour, the cheetah is the world's fastest land animal. The San tell of the race God staged to discover which was the swiftest animal. Cheetah and tsessebe antelope were the favourites. Halfway through the race the tsessebe was well in front and certain to win when it slipped and broke its leg. But instead of claiming victory, the cheetah stopped to help its rival. God was so taken with the cheetah's compassion, say the San, that He gave the cat the power to run faster than any other animal.

Although the cheetah is solitary by nature, visitors to Etosha are more likely to encounter this graceful beast than other predators. The sleekest of Africa's three big cats, the cheetah, with its slender body and long, thin legs, is built for

Above: Flamingo silhouetted against golden sunset in one of Etosha's waterholes.

speed. But the sprint after its prey leaves it so breathless that the intended victim sometimes escapes the capture hold — a claw-raking blow to the flank. At other times, a more dominant killer — lion or hyena — will move in and steal the kill from the still-panting cheetah.

Its docile nature has put the cheetah's future in doubt. In the 1990s the last two remaining strongholds were eastern Africa — Tanzania and Kenya — and southern Africa — Namibia and Botswana. Today, Namibia is known as the cheetah capital of the world as it has the largest remaining population of these cats. On their farm, Okaruikosonduno, near Otjiwarongo, Daniel Kraus and Laurie Marker-Kraus run the Cheetah Preservation Fund, dedicated to ensuring its survival.

Two species of zebra — Hartmann's mountain and Burchell's — roam Etosha's western region, whilst the mountain zebra favours the hills around Otjovasandu in the far south-west. With its white belly and distinctive stripes that continue down the legs to the hoof, this endangered animal is easily distinguished from the common Burchell's zebra.

Where prey congregate, so predators lurk. It is not uncommon to see a pride of lion feasting on Etosha's plains. The high toll of endemic diseases such as anthrax, to which lion are immune, means they often eat without hunting. Between 300 and 400 lions, forming prides of four or more, stalk Etosha, mainly around the waterholes of Halali and Okaukuejo on the southern rim of the pan. The largest of Africa's big cats, lion weigh up to 280 kilos and hunt communally by running down their prey at a top speed of around sixty-five kilometres an hour. Lionesses kill more frequently than males, accounting in an ordinary year for an average nineteen head of game at a weight of about 115 kilos for each kill. The cat's roar, rarely heard during daytime, carries as far as eight kilometres and signals territorial ownership. So powerful is this roar that the beast's breath stirs the dust two metres away. Leopard also stalk Etosha, but these mainly nocturnal animals are rarely seen. They move stealthily through the shadows and rest out of sight during the day.

Much smaller than lion, leopard weigh between thirty and eighty kilos. Killing anything from large antelope or gazelle to small rodents, leopard even eat fish and come as readily to carrion as hyena.

Sweeping 400 kilometres down the Angolan border, the Okavango River flows east to meet the inland delta of Botswana's Okavango Swamp. Where Namibia's broad Kavango plains reach into the Caprivi Strip — along the Zambian border — to the shores of the legendary Zambezi River, the Okavango touches them. The 110,000 people of the Kavango tribe, Namibia's second-largest, which takes its name from the river, represent one-tenth of Namibia's population.

During Angola's long-running civil war many southern Angolan tribes crossed the river to add to their numbers. Not surprisingly, fish is the staple diet of those Kavango who live on Okavango's southern banks. Fisherwomen set their conical wicker traps while their menfolk harpoon the fish from their dugout canoes, *watu*, driven forward by the paddle of a single oarsman. The tribe is matrilineal, tracing its ancestry through female descendants just like their Wambo neighbours.

The Kavango capital of Rundu stands above the fertile floodplains on the south bank of the river, 250 kilometres north-east of Grootfontein. South-west of Rundu, just below the Caprivi Strip, the Kaudom Game Reserve, Namibia's remotest wildlife sanctuary, covers 3,840 square kilometres. This expanse of semi-desert plain is dotted with dry fossil river-beds. Along them roam wild dog, tsessebe, kudu, wildebeest, endangered roan antelope and elephant. During the testing months of the dry season, the elephant tap down into the underground streams that filter west from the Okavango Delta system in

Below: Profusion of water lilies, reeds and papyrus grass flourish in the wilderness wetlands of Namibia's own Okavango Delta in the Caprivi Strip.

Bottom: Tourist camp on Kwando River, Lianshulu. This traditional cottage is fabricated from local materials.

Opposite: Tourists spotting birds from top deck of a floating pontoon on a hidden waterway at Lianshulu, in the Caprivi Strip where the Kwando River flows across the border into the Okavango Delta of Botswana.

Botswana. The presence of the streams under the parched surface is marked by the occasional waterhole which they feed.

Well away from the established tourist trails, facilities in the game reserve — which opened in the middle of the 1980s—- are sparse and basic. No fences bar the ageless game trails. Kaudom's animals are free to roam wherever instinct leads, from one season to the next, in search of new pastures.

The reserve's northern boundary is close to the western gateway into the curious 500-kilometre long, fifty-kilometre wide panhandle of the Caprivi Strip which opens out to sixty-four kilometres across at its eastern end. There Namibia, Botswana, Zambia and Zimbabwe meet in a permanent reminder of Africa's European legacy. At the start of the final decade of the last century the Caprivi Strip was first drawn on the map at the Berlin conference, during the carving up of Africa by the European powers. On 1 July 1890, Britain traded Heligoland and the panhandle for Zanzibar and parts of Bechuanaland, now Botswana. The Caprivi Strip was named after the German Chancellor, General Count Georg Leo von Caprivi di Caprara di Montecuccoli. Almost quarter of a century later, at the very outbreak of the Great War, it was back in British hands — the first German territory to fall. The German district governor had been taking tea with a senior British official from Rhodesia, now Zimbabwe, when the Briton was handed a note to say that war had begun. At once, he placed the German under arrest and annexed the Strip. At the end of the war it was incorporated into Bechuanaland but, at the onset of the Second World War, South Africa assumed control. From 1960, SWAPO established strategic guerrilla strongholds in the Strip, which became a key battleground in the freedom fight against South Africa.

Now all is peaceful and the two main cultures — the Subiya and the Mafwe, who share many similarities with the Kavango — survive unchanged in an area whose remoteness has served as barrier to modern influences. The citizens of East Caprivi are also closely related to neighbouring communities in Zambia, Zimbabwe, Angola and Botswana. As well as common tribal customs and traditions, many also speak the same language. Hunting, fishing, herding cattle and tending crops such as cassava, maize and cereals are central to the Caprivian economy. The Zambezi's seasonal floods are a mixed blessing. They often displace villagers for several months but deposit a rich loamy silt on these marshlands.

The eastern sector near the Zambezi is the most heavily populated area with more than 40,000 people. Many live in and around the regional capital of Katima Mulilo on the banks of the Zambezi River. They reside in small villages of simple mud and wood thatched huts in a culture which has changed little in hundreds of years.

The green, fertile floodplains and perennial wetlands mark much of the

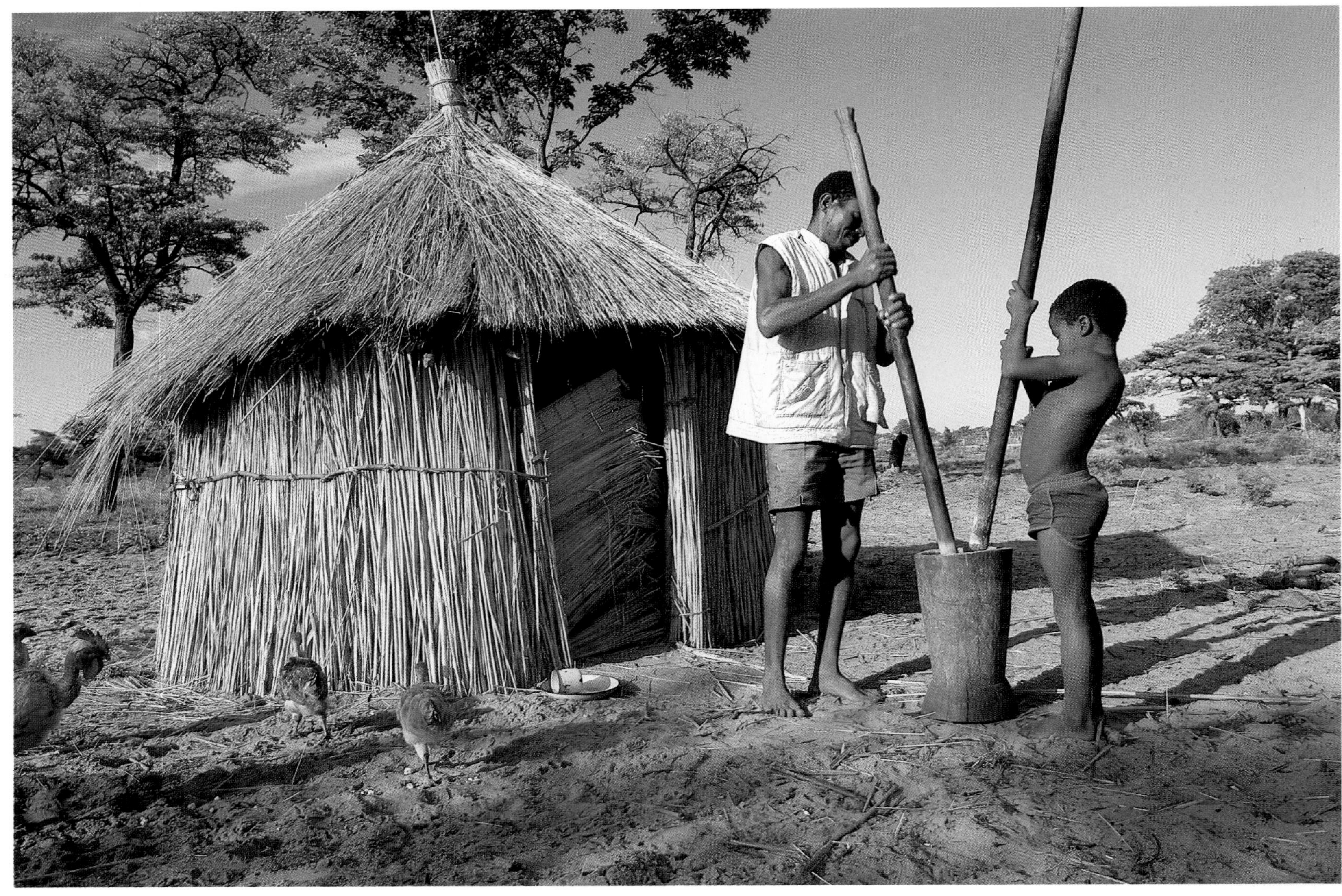

Above: Father and son pounding grain with traditional pestle and mortar in their Namibian homeland at Lizauli, East Caprivi.

Strip's 11,520 square kilometres; and it provides a sharp contrast to the dusty face of the Kalahari. The Caprivi Strip is extremely flat and wherever one goes no part is more than forty-six metres higher than the rest.

Some forty kilometres from the western entrance to the Strip, the Okavango races over the rapids of the Popa Falls, descending sixty-four feet in a series of rocky steps. Over the course of fourteen kilometres it cuts across the Strip to drain into its remarkable delta in the Kalahari. A fishing camp with thatched rustic cabins shaped from teak timber stands by the falls.

Forty kilometres south of the falls, the tributary of the Mahango River marks the northern boundary of the 246 square kilometres of Mahango Game Reserve and Botswana the southern boundary. Visitors trek through the swampland with its contrasting habitats — including indigenous Kalahari teak and copalwood trees to the reedbeds of the Okavango Delta — and more than 300 species of bird. Among the most outstanding birds are the rare, western-banded

Top: Traditional wildlife wood carvings.

Above: Namibia's indigenous woods are used for wildlife carvings and are sold at the roadside.

snake eagle, Pel's fishing owl, white-rumped babbler, African skimmer, swamp boubou, chirping cisticola, finfoot, rock pratincole and the coppery-tailed coucal. The reserve's wildlife include elephant which migrate along the Strip from Angola, Botswana and Zambia during the dry season. There are also many hippo, crocodile and some of southern Africa's most distinctive plains game: blue wildebeest, cape buffalo, kudu, gemsbok, tsessebe, impala, red lechwe, sitatunga, tiny reedbuck, roan and sable — whose magnificent, long, sweeping horns curve backwards. And there are good numbers of wart hog, baboon, ostrich, vervet monkey, lion and leopard.

The jarring, gravel road from Rundu to the Zambezi River snakes through a flat landscape, lush with vegetation including tall elephant grasses. The entire region is virtually one enormous game reserve.

Long before the Strip came into existence the area was home to a multiplicity of warring cultures. The Subiya, who occupied the land in the east between the Chobe and Zambezi Rivers, dominated the region 400 years ago. At the end of the seventeenth century, Sundano, the Subiyan ruler, set out to enlarge his kingdom. He seized large parts of what is now southern Zambia to found the ruling dynasty which continues to this day.

The Yezi clan, which broke away from their Botswana kin to settle in the Strip, also wielded considerable influence during the eighteenth and early nineteenth centuries. The Scottish explorer and missionary David Livingstone records in 1849 that they were ruled by a chief named Lechulatebe.

Of all these tribes, however, only the Fwe live solely within the borders of the Caprivi Strip and, although their culture is similar to the Kavango, little else is known of them except that they are believed to have migrated from the north through Kavango. The region's martial history is still recounted by tribal elders who recall the heroic deeds of such warriors as Mwanambinyi, who ruled Barotseland 300 years ago. He defeated Lukonga of the Mbukushu — the echo of his victory has rung down through the centuries — across the emptiness of Caprivi's open prairies. Known as Itenge before, East Caprivi was ruled almost continuously by the Lozi who commanded twenty-five tribes at the start of the nineteenth century. The greatest of all Lozi kings was Mulambwa, the great commander, king of kings, lawmaker and judge.

Stability came to an end in 1820, the Time of Troubles, *Difagane*, when an influx of refugees from Shaka the Zulu moved northwards across southern Africa's highveld. At the same time, marauding invaders also moved northwards across the Limpopo, leaving havoc in their wake.

The Kololo, a Sotho tribe, were among the most aggressive, wandering for years across southern Africa waging war against everyone they met. When they marched through the Okavango Delta into East Caprivi they were led by the great Sebitwane. After overthrowing the Lozi king, and forcing the Lozi into the

Previous Pages: Caprivi Strip fisherman poles dugout canoe along a reed-lined backwater of the Kwando River.

Above: Tour group surveys the tranquil wetlands of Namibia's lush Caprivi Strip.

swamps of Zambia, Sebitwane appointed sub-chiefs and built new villages in his kingdom. He then invited Livingstone to bring the word of God to the Caprivi Strip. When the king died in 1851, Livingstone was with him. Soon after, the Lozi returned and slaughtered Sebitwane's successor.

In the centre of the panhandle, sandwiched between Angola and Botswana, the Strip's flat, fertile floodplain forms the Caprivi Game Reserve. Together with two smaller reserves it serves as the stage for some of Africa's greatest wildlife spectacles. Caprivi teems with prolific numbers of roan antelope, kudu, blue wildebeest, giraffe, hippo, Burchell's zebra and elephant. Although many other species browse in the park's woodlands, the largest congregations assemble around the Kwando River which flows across the strip to the Okavango Delta and marks the park's western perimeter. The Malombe and Ndwasa pans at the centre of the park lure animals during the dry season. The village of Kongola lies on the edge of the park.

Top: Vibrant colours of the sharp-beaked little bee-eater. Above: Masked weaver performs dazzling avian antics.

Forty-five kilometres north-east of Caprivi Game Reserve, rare wetlands and expansive woodlands were preserved in 1990 as Mudumu National Park. The yearly rainfall sometimes exceeds a metre. As well as its western wetlands, treasured ecosystems in arid southern Africa, the park has extensive mopane and terminalia woodlands. Visitors wander through its sylvan trails on foot, taking care not to disturb the elephants that browse there.

Three rivers — the Kwando, Linyanti and Zambezi — give eastern Caprivi, which has the country's highest rainfall, its distinctive character. They form the borders between Namibia and its neighbours. The waters of the Linyanti and Zambezi feed the shallow depths of Lake Liambesi, which covers more than 100 square kilometres. It is never deeper than five metres and is surrounded by 200 square kilometres of swampland. It loses large surface areas every year to evaporation. In fact, the lake vanished altogether during the savage drought of 1985 and the local fisherfolk, who harvest a tonne of fish a day in good times, were suddenly starving. The area where the Kwando and Linyanti Rivers hurry to their meeting on the Botswana border is conserved as the Mamili National Park, which was also established in 1990. It is formed around two large islands, Nkasa and Lupala, in Namibia's own smaller version of the Okavango Delta — a region of reed-lined waterways rich in wildlife and birdlife. In wet years, large areas are flooded and become accessible only by boat.

Katima Mulilo, the Caprivi capital which stands on the banks of the great Zambezi River at the easternmost point of the Strip, is one of the most intriguing towns in Africa.

The colourful market offers fish, fresh food, brightly-coloured garments and locally crafted soapstone curios and wood carvings. The town's luxury tourist lodge with golf course, swimming pool and thatched cottages, has a floating bar moored in the Zambezi. Tourists sip cocktails while watching the river's hippo and giant crocodile. The lodge actually began life as a simple boarding house for visiting engineers. It was erected by Gert Visagie, a construction engineer who settled at Katima Mulilo in the late 1970s, after undertaking a nine-month contract there. It quickly grew into the luxurious Zambezi Lodge, spread along the Zambezi's tree-shaded banks. Since his arrival, Visagie has played a major role in the region's development. He built an arts centre and gave it to the local Namibian artists under the management of playwright, potter, artist and folklorist Moses Nasilele.

Visagie has also been behind the construction of schools, hospital, post office and bush clinics. But his real triumph is the floating restaurant that became the forty-four-metre-long river boat, *Zambezi Queen*. He designed it and spent a year building the vessel. The only holiday cruiser on southern Africa's inland waters, the *Zambezi Queen* has thirteen staterooms, an exotic honeymoon suite, two lounges, dining room and an entertainment deck.

Above: Honeycomb of carmine bee-eater nests eats into the crumbling banks of the Kwando River which flows from Angola across the Caprivi Strip into the Okavango Delta.

When the river rises after the rains, Visagie becomes skipper on four- to eight-day cruises with his crew of eight sailing south down the Zambezi to the top of the mighty Victoria Falls.

The river teems with some of the finest freshwater game fish in the world — tiger, western bottlenose, tilapia and brownspot largemouth — while the skies are filled with a rich diversity of birdlife, among them fish eagles, bee-eaters and kingfishers.

And the town has a unique claim to fame — one that should inspire caution. Katima Mulilo is the only town in the world where elephants have right of way as they parade daily along the capital's streets to water on the river bank.

Truly, this land of lost horizons is a remote and beautiful wilderness. And as the sun sinks below the meandering course of the Zambezi, the words of a Bushman poem, recorded by Laurens van der Post in *The Lost World of the*

Above: Golden sundown over the tree-shaded banks of the great Zambezi River.

Kalahari, linger in the soft evening air evoking the wonder of a *Journey through Namibia.*

Oh! Listen to the wind,
You woman there;
The time is coming,
The rain is near.
Listen to your heart,
Your hunter is here.